BEFORE THE

# POINT

OF

# NO

# RETURN

# BEFORE THE
# POINT
## OF
# NO
# RETURN

## An Exchange of Views on the Cold War, the Reagan Doctrine, and What Is to Come

Leon Litwack • Stephen F. Cohen • Arthur Macy Cox
Robert Scheer • Edward P. Thompson • Martin Sherwin
George W. Breslauer • Leon Wofsy • Diana Johnstone
Michael T. Klare • Patricia Flynn • Tom Wicker
Stanley Hoffmann • Strobe Talbott • Hans A. Bethe
Noam Chomsky • Paul M. Sweezy • Flora Lewis
Rev. Theodore M. Hesburgh • Barbara Epstein
Michael MccGwire • Gil Green • Manning Marable
Malcolm W. Gordon • Marcus G. Raskin

edited by Leon Wofsy

MONTHLY REVIEW PRESS
NEW YORK

"A Matter of Global Survival" first appeared in the *Nation*, 12 October 1985, copyright © 1985 by Stephen F. Cohen; "The Sources of American Conduct" first appeared in *Socialist Review*, no. 80 (1985), copyright © 1985 by Martin J. Sherwin. Both are reprinted with permission.

*Library of Congress Cataloging in Publication Data*

Before the point of no return.
    1. United States—Foreign relations—1981–
2. World politics—1975–1985.   I. Litwack, Leon F.
II. Wofsy, Leon.
E876.B44   1986     327.73      86-18263
ISBN 0-85345-714-X
ISBN 0-85345-713-1 (pbk.)

Monthly Review Press
155 West 23rd Street
New York, N.Y. 10011

10 9 8 7 6 5 4 3 2 1

# Contents

# Preface

This volume is the result of a project on Alternatives to Cold War conducted from 1983 to 1986 under grants from the University of California's Institute on Global Conflict and Cooperation and the California Council for the Humanities. The focus of the project was explained in the initiating proposal:

> While there is much current research and debate on issues of arms control *per se*, our [project] would center attention on the Cold War context that dictates continuation of the arms race. We believe that real forward motion to end the arms race will depend finally on both public and governmental willingness, here and in the USSR, to rethink deeply imbedded Cold War propositions.

In 1983, despite widespread alarm about the danger of nuclear catastrophe, there was almost no public discussion about changing the Cold War impasse in U.S.-Soviet relations, perhaps because it seemed so irrevocable. There is somewhat more attention now. President Reagan and General Secretary Gorbachev have met at the summit, but "deeply imbedded Cold War propositions" still prevail without serious challenge in our politics and culture. The arms race moves further out of control in a treacherous environment of undiminished crisis and conflict.

The conferences, seminars, and correspondence organized by our project brought out differing views and perceptions even among severe critics of Cold War policies. Most of the material presented in Part I: The Cold War World was culled from contributions to two conferences, in June 1983 and November 1984, and to a symposium held in September 1983. Except for a few visitors from Britain and Latin America, participants were from the United

States; none were attached to the governments of the United States or the Soviet Union.

Selected talks and lectures were transcribed from tapes and excerpted for publication. The Cox, Scheer, Breslauer (in part), and Klare contributions were part of the June 1983 conference; Thompson's contribution is excerpted from a lecture co-sponsored by Alternatives to Cold War and the San Francisco Media Center in July 1983; Flynn and Wicker participated in the September 1983 symposium; and the contributions by Sherwin, Breslauer (in part), Johnstone and myself were part of the November 1984 conference. Stephen Cohen's contribution, which appeared in the *Nation* of 12 October 1985 has been included as the first piece in this volume because he states so clearly a key premise that motivated our undertaking: "The greatest failure of American democracy today is the absence of a real national debate on U.S. policy toward the Soviet Union."

In selecting from the many contributions to our conferences, I have avoided reproducing discussion of specific matters that time and events have pushed aside during the three eventful years of project activities. The choice has been to highlight varying analyses of questions that bear most directly on prospects for a shift away from the Cold War: What is the Cold War, what is it about? What are the goals of either side? How much depends on who happens to be in the White House, who in the Kremlin? Are there factors, international and domestic, that can lessen the dominance of the Great Contest over the course of human events?

Part II: The Future of the Cold War presents responses to two questions, solicited from a number of people between October 1985 and May 1986. The questions were:

- *Do you think peaceful termination of the Cold War is a real possibility in the foreseeable future?*
- *If so, under what circumstances?*

This correspondence was undertaken because we felt that most comments on the Cold War avoid critical analysis of the prospects for ending it. Our project conferences, stimulating as they were, did not overcome this deficiency. All of our discussions emphasized how dangerous the Cold War is, and prevailing policies were sharply condemned. Yet there seemed to be some feeling—although not overtly expressed and debated—that the United States and the Soviet Union are incapable, as both societies now exist, of departing significantly from the catastrophic arms race or from their overall Cold War relationships. This is so basic a consideration—so much depends on whether or not that estimate is valid—that we wanted to hold it up to direct scrutiny.

The answers we received were divergent in content and in form. There were letters and essays; some dealt with the questions directly, while others developed aspects of relevant problems. There were striking conflicts of opinion. In provoking such debate, my reasoning is that effective peace effort depends on more than a strong mixture of fear and hope about the future. Motivation must come also through evidence, in thought and in action, that humanity is capable of overcoming the threat of extinction.

Choosing a title for this volume turned out to be a debate in itself. The initial choice was *The Cold War: Can There Be a Peaceful Ending?* but dissenters said the Cold War has been with us so long that "another book with a Cold War title would seem boring." The present title, *Before the Point of No Return,* should perhaps be followed by a question mark, since some contributors suggest we may now be at or past that point, but my own prejudice is that hope and reality are still compatible.

My thanks go to all who made the Alternatives to Cold War project and this volume possible. The colleagues who joined me in submitting the original proposal were George Breslauer, Barbara Epstein, Leon Litwack, and Reginald Zelnik. In addition to support from the granting agencies (named at the outset), there was generous administrative assistance from the Institute for International Studies and the Institute for the Study of Social Change, both on the University of California's Berkeley campus, the Center for Social Research and Education in Berkeley, and the Institute for Policy Studies in Washington, D.C.

Barbara Epstein and Michael Klare helped plan most project endeavors and did preliminary editing of material from the first conference. George Breslauer, Reginald Zelnik, and Richard Walker were indispensable to the success of the first conference; Jeff Escoffier, Greg McLaughlin, and Karen Hansen contributed similarly to the second. Pravin Varaiya arranged our symposium on

Central America and Troy Duster set up an informal discussion with the Hon. Andrew Young. We thank all who took part in project events.

Encouragement for this book has come from the Program on Peace and Conflict Studies, University of California, Berkeley, which confirmed the need for a reader to supplement what is now offered in courses on peace, security, and U.S.-Soviet relations. I thank Susan Lowes, director of Monthly Review Press, for her valuable guidance in putting the volume together. The highly competent contribution of Kathie Campbell in preparing the manuscript is much appreciated. Thanks go also to Roz Wofsy, L.W.'s most persistent and helpful critic.

*Leon Wofsy*

*June 1986*

# LEON F. LITWACK

Professor of History, University of California, Berkeley;
President, Organization of American Historians

# Introduction

Three weeks after the end of World War II, President Harry
Truman told the American people that they possessed "the greatest strength and the greatest power which man has ever reached."
He did not exaggerate. By contrast, the Soviet Union had lost 20
million dead, much of its richest land had been devastated, and its
industrial capacity had been cut by nearly 50 percent. For Americans, accustomed to seeing the future as an improved version of
the present, it was a time of self-congratulation and great expectations. The twentieth century, said Henry Luce of *Life* and *Time,*
would surely be the American century. No less ebullient, liberal
columnist Max Lerner proclaimed the United States the "only
fabulous country," and historian Daniel Boorstin was moved to
ask, "Why should we make a five-year plan for ourselves when God
seems to have had a thousand-year plan ready-made for us?"

But within two years, the American people found themselves in
a situation for which there were no apparent historical precedents:
a Cold War, based on the perceived threat of a monstrous international conspiracy bent on world conquest and the destruction of
the "American Way of Life." For the impact it would have on U.S.
society, politics, culture, and the economy, the fear of the Soviet
Union and Communist aggression and subversion ranks among
the most extraordinary and far-reaching developments in U.S.
history. Not only did it distort the economy and paralyze politics,
but it eroded the tradition of dissent and critical inquiry.

The psychology of the Cold War became so deeply entrenched in
Washington, D.C., in the nation's press, in academia, in the trade
union movement, and in the minds of most Americans that only

one point of view survived. To debate the assumptions on which the Cold War was based, to question the constant and inevitable danger of Soviet military and ideological aggression, to challenge the validity of official perceptions of Soviet behavior was to seem indifferent to the nation's very safety. Debate was effectively stilled, anti-Communism became the definitive test of patriotism, and an entire generation of dissidents was excluded from positions of public responsibility and influence.

The consensus and mobilization usually demanded for the prosecution of a war was demanded after 1947 for the prosecution of U.S. foreign policy. The president articulated the growing U.S.-Soviet confrontation with a rhetoric that virtually precluded debate: "Our homes, our Nation, all the things we believe in are in great danger. We must not be confused about the issue which confronts the world today. It is tyranny or freedom. And even *worse,* Communism denies the very existence of God."

The threat of an alien presence within the United States was brought home in such a way that it became increasingly difficult to distinguish between fact and fantasy, between Hollywood's *The Red Nightmare, The Red Menace, Red Planet Mars,* and *Invasion of the Body Snatchers* and the warning in 1950 of President Truman's attorney general that Communist conspirators reached into the very fiber of U.S. life: "The Communists in America are everywhere—in factories, offices, butcher shops, on street corners, in private business—and each carries in himself the germs of death for society." Joseph McCarthy had not yet made his political debut as an anti-Communist crusader, but he learned from others, Democrats and Republicans alike, how to exploit the issue of Communist subversion for political profit and advancement.

The Truman Doctrine made absolutely clear the U.S. rational for the Cold War: "Totalitarian regimes imposed on free peoples, by direct or indirect aggression, undermine the foundations of international peace and hence the security of the United States." The message to Congress on March 12, 1947, read very much like a declaration of ideological warfare. Each nation was asked to make its choice between freedom and tyranny, between light and darkness. For the next quarter century, that doctrine would profoundly shape the conduct of U.S. foreign relations. "From Korea to Berlin to Cuba to Vietnam," Senator William Fulbright would write, "the Truman Doctrine governed America's response to the Communist world. Tactics changed—from 'massive retaliation' to 'limited war' and 'counter-insurgency'—but these were variations on a classic formulation that few questioned."

Forty years and eight presidents later, after the expenditure of billions of dollars, 33,000 lives in Korea and 56,000 lives in Vietnam, Americans are less secure than when they embarked upon their quest for national and internal security. The rhetoric is all too familiar, dividing the world irreconcilably into camps of good and evil, based on the same assumptions of an evil Communist conspiracy and a unique American virtue and destiny. "I've always believed that this land was placed here between the two great oceans by some divine plan," Ronald Reagan observed. "It was placed there to be found by a special kind of people. We built a new breed of human, called an American. We can meet our destiny, and that destiny is to build a land here that will be for all mankind a shining city on a hill."

Like the heroes he admired in Hollywood films, Ronald Reagan wanted to make Uncle Sam once again respected and feared in the world community. And the heroes he admired made no deals with villains; they vanquished them. The inauguration had hardly ended before Reagan unleashed a verbal attack on the Soviet Union that had not been heard since the early years of the Cold War. In his first press conference, he said the Russians could not be trusted because "they reserve unto themselves the right to commit any crime, to lie, to cheat" in order to achieve world domination. The Soviet Union, Reagan insisted, "underlies all the unrest" in the world, and he underscored the differences between the two great superpowers in a rhetoric that almost plagiarized Truman's: "They don't subscribe to our sense of morality because they don't believe in any of the good things; they don't believe in an afterlife. They don't believe in a God or a religion, and . . . the only morality they recognize, therefore, is what will advance the cause of socialism." In a speech to fundamentalist preachers in Orlando, Florida, Reagan excoriated the Soviet Union as "an evil empire" and sounded the theme of Holy War, calling upon his audience to enlist in his crusade: "There is sin and evil in the world and we are enjoined by Scriptures and the Lord Jesus to oppose it with all our might." He used the same source to justify his arms buildup: "You might be interested to know that the Scriptures are on our side in this."

The illusions which we Americans have embraced since World War II about our role and destiny are not, in fact, unique. Neither the United States nor the Soviet Union seem to have understood fully the revolutionary upheavals transforming much of the world, including peoples who for centuries had been consigned to colonial or semicolonial status. Neither power has faced up to the growing irrelevance of its example. More often than not, the principal victims of the Cold War have been those very peoples with whom the superpowers wished to share the blessings of their system. The United States and the Soviet Union have often seemed like inadvertent fellow travelers, each in its own way seeking to defy or thwart the forces of social change: the United States in Southeast Asia and Central America, the Soviet Union in Czechoslovakia, Poland, and Afghanistan.

To place the blame for the Cold War, its origins and persistence, on either the United States or the Soviet Union would be to simplify and distort much of the history of that conflict. No single view of the Cold War brings the contributors to this volume together, only the felt need to rethink deeply held Cold War propositions and assumptions, only the urgent need to find ways to end this costly, unproductive, and unwinnable conflict. For forty years, it has persisted, pervading nearly every sector of our society. The obsession with national security and internal subversion has consumed billions of dollars and the allocation of immense resources for the elaboration of weapons of destruction. It has necessitated a reordering of national priorities, the mobilization of various agencies of government. It has encouraged pacts and alliances with numerous countries, and it has required intervention—overt and clandestine—in internal disputes around the world. None of the Founding Fathers could have even contemplated these developments some two hundred years ago, when they met in Philadelphia to form "a more perfect union, establish justice, insure domestic tranquility, provide for the common defense, promote the general welfare, and secure the blessings of liberty to ourselves and our posterity."

In the 1980s, Americans remain imprisoned in their quest for ultimate security. The Reagan administration purchases, deploys, and contemplates still more sophisticated systems. But with each new generation of nuclear weapons, the ultimate result has been to diminish rather than enhance the national security. This diminished security has in turn justified another round of weapons. "We have gone on piling . . . new levels of destructiveness upon old ones," George Kennan wrote. "We have done this helplessly, almost involuntarily: like the victims of some sort of hypnotism. . . . We have achieved, we and the Russians together, . . . levels of redundancy of such grotesque dimensions as to defy rational understanding." Where will it end? Himself one of the authors of the containment policy in the late 1940s, George Kennan has come to conclude, "There is no issue at stake in our political relations with the Soviet Union—no hope, no fear, nothing to which we aspire, nothing we would like to avoid—which could conceivably be worth a nuclear war."

Public opinion polls suggest that a significant majority of Americans would also prefer a less dangerous course. This collection, *Before the Point of No Return,* addresses that preference, believing it possible to reexamine the Cold War in new and meaningful ways and to question the ingrained habits and assumptions of the policymakers. The alternative to such questioning is already being realized: an arms race whose uncontrolled momentum threatens to destroy humankind or render this nation an armory empty of human compassion and indifferent to humanist goals and concerns.

In recent years, loyalty and patriotism have become confused with a mindless, flag-waving, orchestrated chorus of "U.S.A." Throughout its history, this nation has thrived on dissent and moral inquiry. Its indispensable strength has been freedom of expression—freedom to question and probe various versions of reality. The highest kind of patriotism, true loyalty to one's country, may demand disloyalty to its pretenses, hostility to the policies of its government, a willingness to unmask its leaders, and a recognition of the limits of its power. History should teach us that it is not the rebels or dissidents who endanger a society but rather the accepting, the unthinking, the unquestioning, the silent, the indifferent. This lesson knows no national boundaries. And it is in that spirit that we present this collection, inviting your interest, dialogue, involvement, and dissent.

# THE
# COLD
# WAR
# WORLD

## PART 1

# STEPHEN F. COHEN

Professor of Politics, Princeton University;
columnist, *Nation*

# A Matter of Global Survival

The greatest failure of American democracy today is the absence of a real national debate on U.S. policy toward the Soviet Union. No international or domestic issue is more important, and nothing in the foreseeable future—including the Reagan-Gorbachev summit meeting—will change that fact. In the nuclear age, the nature of the U.S.-Soviet relationship is a matter of global survival. And as government defense-related spending soars toward $400 billion a year, Cold War relations increasingly and inescapably erode the quality of American life, from education and Social Security to urban housing and agriculture.

Despite all these ramifications, President Reagan's Cold War policy has gone essentially unchallenged in the political mainstream for almost five years. Critics have lamented the administration's extremist rhetoric, protested some of its weapons programs, and doubted its commitment to arms control. But not one influential group or institution has mounted a sustained opposition to Reagan's militarized approach to the Soviet Union, either by rejecting its underlying political premises or by offering the only alternative, a broad policy of détente.

As a result, in contrast to wide-ranging controversies over other issues, mainstream discussion of U.S.-Soviet relations is narrow and superficial. It fixates on trivial or secondary matters, such as pre-summit "public relations" and the efficacy of yet another weapons system, while avoiding fundamental questions about the long-term goal of U.S. policy. Is it to live peacefully with the Soviet Union as an equal superpower? To roll back Soviet power in the world? To destroy the Soviet system? No coherent policy is possible without answers to these and other questions about the kind of relationship the United States wants. They are not even being discussed.

The entire U.S. political spectrum bears responsibility for this failure of the democratic process. The right is mindlessly committed to Cold War, including military build-up, as an eternal virtue. The left is instinctively opposed to the arms race but has no ideas for achieving the broader political accords needed to end it. And the vaunted "bipartisan center" wishes only to stand safely somewhere between.

More specifically, there is the baneful role of the national media, the Democratic Party, and the legion of professional foreign policy intellectuals. Each has some capacity, as well as duty, to broaden and deepen public discourse about U.S.-Soviet relations. Not one has done so.

Ten years ago, newspaper editorial pages and network television programs regularly featured proponents and opponents of détente. Now, overwhelmingly, they present only representatives of the Cold War right and the center, typically a supporter of the administration and a self-described "defense Democrat." In addition, the recent practice, as on ABC's "Nightline," of casting a Soviet official in the role of primary anti-Reagan spokesman, implies that there is no legitimate U.S. position anywhere between them.

The media's culpability may be mostly passive, but nothing so kind can be said about the Democratic Party. Even though Reagan's military expenditures have savaged the party's social programs, it offered no alternative to his Soviet policy in 1984 and seems determined not to do so in future elections. One party politician and advisor after another has rejected an electoral platform based on détente, which is necessary to free funds for social progress, clamoring instead for a more anti-Soviet, pro-defense program. If a Cold War manifesto by liberal Representative Stephen J. Solarz, in the *New York Times* of 20 June 1985, is any indication, that program will be a replica of Reagan's.

Nor can anything positive be said in this respect about foreign policy intellectuals with access to the media and to the Democratic Party. If such people have a useful function, it is to think unconventionally and to speak more candidly than politicians. A great many policy intellectuals are sincere cold warriors, but many others must believe in the necessity and possibility of détente, as they said openly and often in the 1970s. Why do so few of them speak out now?

The main reason is well known but rarely publicized. Like too many Congressional Democrats (and perhaps Republicans) who will not state publicly what they express privately, they are intimidated by the renewed Cold War climate of political intolerance, especially on Soviet affairs.

Debate is again being stifled by censorious crusaders parading under euphemistic banners like the Committee for the Free World, Accuracy in Media, and Accuracy in Academia. Once again, a galaxy of Cold War publications recklessly brand anyone who dissents as being pro-Soviet, soft on Communism, a fellow traveler, or an appeaser. Such intolerance has even crept into some once civil-tongued newspapers and magazines. Not long ago, a *New York Post* editorial accused ABC of "doing Yuri Andropov's job." And the *New Republic* said of a leading U.S. expert on the Soviet Union, "With such Sovietologists, who needs the Soviets?"

And yet, given the overriding importance of U.S.-Soviet relations, it is impossible to sympathize with believers in détente who fall silent or muffle their criticism of U.S. policy with platitudes about "bipartisan consensus," a "responsible center," and being "tough with the Soviets." Compared with the cost of political courage in other societies, the American price is cheap. Pro-détente senators who refuse to lead should step down. Policy intellectuals who prepare recipes for consumer taste should become cooks. And government officials who dissent from cold war policy only under a pseudonym, as one did in the *New York Times* in 1982, should resign.

Cold warriors will exclaim, as they always do, "Everything is worse in the Soviet Union!"—as if that should be America's standard. But no one can take pride in the fact that the nation's largest political problem is not begin debated. Democratic discourse requires candor, courage, and civility, and all three are woefully lacking.

# ARTHUR MACY COX

Author; member, Board of Directors,
American Committee on East-West Accord

## Cold War Versus Détente

During the first stage of U.S. Cold War policy, the State Department devised a national policy statement that became known as "National Security Council Policy 68," or NSC-68. I think I will read two sections from that policy, because these two sections represent something that has been consistently endorsed in one way or another by the leaders in our government ever since 1950, when this was written. The first was that the major goal of U.S. policy would be "to foster the seeds of destruction within the Soviet system so that the Kremlin is brought at least to the point of modifying its behavior to generally acceptable international standards." The second is, "Without superior aggregate military strength in being and readily mobilizable, a policy of containment, which is in effect a policy of calculated and gradual coercion, is no more than a policy of bluff." In other words, we needed the assets to take the struggle right to the backyard of the Soviet Union, and we also needed the military power necessary to follow a policy of calculated and gradual coercion. Now it is very interesting that these two fundamental objectives have been brought back almost precisely in these terms by the Reagan administration, in a new policy statement that was adopted a year ago and leaked to the *New York Times*.

After Stalin's death, change began to occur in the Soviet Union and Khrushchev brought a new approach to many things. I was one of the small group assigned to go out to the Marine training base at Quantico, Virginia, with Nelson Rockefeller to plan for our first summit with the Soviet Union—the Geneva summit of 1955. And it was fascinating to see the debate that went on. There were

22

about twenty or twenty-five men who were participating and planning the U.S. role in this agenda. It soon became clear that there were those who wanted to stick only to these policies that I just read—to the Cold War policies—and those who were more flexible, who said, "Here is Khrushchev making certain overtures. We should take very opportunity we can to foster and encourage and promote those developments within the Soviet system that could move us toward a growing détente, a growing relaxation of tension and the avoidance of confrontation and war." This process, in my opinion, has continued from 1955 to the present. It has been a contest between those who are broadly referred to as "détentists" and those who are referred to as "cold warriors." The cold warriors, for various reasons, have wanted the Cold War to continue. They have always opposed things that could reduce tension, and the détentists have been wont to pursue options and developments that could reduce tension.

Some progress was made toward détente under Khrushchev. Then, of course, the Hungarian uprising occurred, and when it was crushed there was a great setback to the kinds of experiments that Khrushchev had been engaging in. One of the ironies about the Hungarian thing was that that revolution might have succeeded—at least to the point of being a Titoist liberalization of the Hungarian system—had it not been for the invasion of Suez by British, French, and Israeli forces. Suslov and Mikoyan were in Budapest under instructions that had been worked out between Khrushchev and Mao Tsetung to negotiate the withdrawal of the Red Army. And, in fact, the Red Army had begun withdrawing when everything was turned around. Ever since, we have had ebbs and flows in the process of East and West getting together and working out arrangements that would make some more sense.

Khrushchev came to the United States in 1958 and met with General Eisenhower at Camp David, where they clearly were on the way to a deal. Eisenhower, as you may know, was the greatest World War II hero in the Soviet Union other than Marshall Zhukov. He was revered. Khrushchev and Eisenhower agreed that they would have a summit meeting in Paris. And after that successful summit meeting, Eisenhower would then go to the Soviet Union and tour the great cities, from coast to coast. But it didn't happen because of the U-2 incident and Gary Powers being shot down.

We have had this kind of thing through the years—ups and downs, beginning to get a little closer and then, for varying reasons, some of them almost fateful, we have pulled back, pulled away. Usually, in my opinion, the hawks have reinforced the hawks on both sides. The hawks have not wanted our two societies to get closer together. They have not wanted a relaxation of tensions. And various things have been done on both sides that have screwed things up.

We saw in Kennedy's years, with the Cuban missile crisis, another dramatic opportunity for change. Kennedy in his last year was, in my opinion, moving for a real détente. His American University speech is worth rereading. The partial test ban agreement, the hotline agreement, were steps toward détente. Then came Vietnam under Johnson, followed by a real change, a real political change, in the United States. Meanwhile Willy Brandt, Chancellor of the Federal Republic of Germany, took what I think were the most important steps toward real détente that have occurred since World War II, when he negotiated the nonintervention pact with the Soviet Union, which opened up diplomatic relations with Poland and Czechoslovakia and, most important, recognized East Germany as a separate state. This was followed by the four-power agreement on Berlin, so that the tremendous tensions that had existed in central Europe were dramatically reduced, and communications between East and West Germany opened up. Trade grew rapidly, and this was followed, as you know, by the 1972 summit in Moscow which Nixon and Kissinger pushed forward with their stated policy of moving toward negotiations and away from confrontation.

Of course, the Soviets have made a number of blunders along the way. They are terribly handicapped by a secrecy and paranoia about their security that is, in my opinion, excessive but very real. They also still dabble with an ideology that sets them back in one way after another. This began with the sending of Cuban troops into Angola and again into Ethiopia and Yemen, and, finally, the Afghanistan invasion. All of these things gave credibility to forces in the United States that wanted to restore the Cold War. The

Committee on the Present Danger began to have tremendous credibility all over the country, so that the Democratic Party was badly split—the neoconservatives and the conservative elements of the party on the one hand, and the moderates and liberals on the other. And, gradually, as the Carter administration moved forward, Zbigniew Brzezinski became dominant. His position as a cold warrior carried more authority while the détentists were badly defeated—people like Cyrus Vance, Paul Warnke, Leslie Gelb, and Marshall Shulman. At the end, most of them resigned. And those who remained were virtually impotent, so that we saw at the end of the Carter administration a real restoration of the Cold War. Thus we had Presidential Directive No. 59, which was the first time a president of the United States had signed a policy statement directing us to prepare to fight and win a "limited nuclear war," and to have the weapons necessary for that. The MX was part of that process. Most of the weapons systems that you see being developed by the Reagan administration were originally launched under the Carter administration, under a group of policy advisors who were advocates of restoring the Cold War. Some of them are what I call "unreconstructed cold warriors"; others newer to the game became persuaded by the Soviet actions in Africa and Afghanistan that we really did need a return to a Cold War.

Now we have the Reagan administration and, for the first time in our history, we have a group of people in power who come from the far right of the U.S. political spectrum. These people are what I call ideologues. They are people who have an ideology which calls for bringing the Soviet Union to its knees one way or another, and, if necessary, preparing to fight them and defeat them in a nuclear war. We have a policy that calls for us to have the capacity to "decapitate" the Soviet state. What does "decapitate" mean? It means that we should have weapons so accurate, so powerful, and so fast on target that they can eliminate the Soviet civilian and military leadership in a matter of minutes, and can knock out the Soviet communications systems in such a way that they cannot counterattack. That means, in other words, that the whole concept that we have been living with for years, the concept of deterrence, the knowledge by both sides that the other side could respond to a first strike with a second strike that would be totally incapacitating, would come to an end. That is the dream behind this policy. Some of the weapons systems that we are developing now will come close to fulfilling that dream. I have talked to people who think that this can really happen. And, of course, the Soviets are absolutely terrified about this.

There is no doubt in my mind that they are absolutely serious about their terror, because the most vulnerable and fragile aspect of nuclear weapons systems is their command and control and communications systems. When the Reagan administration came in and took a look at the fragility of our systems, they decided to ask Congress for $20 billion to try to build a system that would be sufficiently secure to protect us from the prospects of accidental and unintentional nuclear war. And the Soviets are far behind us in computer technology. Their command and control systems are much more vulnerable than ours. Ours make frequent errors—we had three national nuclear alerts in one eighteen-month period. Fortunately, we had time to discover that they were false alarms. But in the future, as this technology advances, we are not going to have the time. As Fred Ikle, the present undersecretary of defense for policy, says, "The noose tightening around our neck is the fact that we will not have enough time to determine how to respond." This becomes especially true if we do something so insane as to place MX missiles in Minuteman-III silos, where they become a target for immediate elimination; and almost certainly because of that we will have to go to what is called *launch on warning*—that means you launch your weapons on first warning of a nuclear attack. And that is a very risky thing when you consider that we do have these errors in our warning systems. And the Soviets have even more errors. The Pershing II that we put into the Federal Republic of Germany in late 1983 can reach Soviet targets in about eight minutes. Could you imagine any kind of human system that could possibly be responsive to an eight-minute attack?

[. . .] So we are moving, unbelievably, into a position where we force the Soviets into a corner from which accidental, unintentional nuclear war increasingly becomes a likelihood. These are the great dangers of the policies being pursued by the zealots in the White House today. And, in my opinion, the only thing that can be done about this is to change the policies and to move toward

serious negotiation with the Soviet Union. I have no doubt—
absolutely no doubt—that the Soviets are prepared to negotiate
very seriously on the control of nuclear weapons, and to move in
the direction of greater stability rather than instability.

# ROBERT SCHEER

Author; journalist, *Los Angeles Times*

# The Cold War Revived

Ten years ago, we would not have thought there would be such a conference as this. During the Nixon years we thought that the Cold War was sort of winding down. In fact, what you heard around campus then was a left analysis of the two superpowers dividing up the world, a left suspicion of the whole process. There wasn't much interest in the questions that now interest people—nuclear war, the superpower rivalry, and so forth. And it seems to me a measure of how far we have come that we once again have to consider "alternatives to the Cold War."

My view of the current situation can be described quite simply. I think that we have experienced the collapse of the center. I think that we of the New Left in the 1960s made a mistake in our evaluation of the forces in this society. I think we exaggerated the strength of the center. I think we exaggerated the vitality and cohesion of liberalism—or what used to be called corporate liberalism—as an ideology. I think we exaggerated the coherence of a ruling class or ruling elite or establishment and the ability of that establishment to pursue its rational interests. It seems to me that the last coherent statement that we have had of a centrist, establishment point of view in this society was provided by the Nixon administration, which at that point was in disarray. And now a counter-ideology is in fact in power. I feel quite strongly that we have to get used to the idea that we have not had yet another pragmatic shift in U.S. politics, that we have not had another candidate who said one thing while he was running and then when he came into office brought in a bipartisan coalition, moved to the center—all of those things that we expect from U.S. politicians.

We expect them to be pragmatic, cynical, centrists. It seems quite the opposite with the Reagan administration. Reagan has, in fact, been true to his ideology, an ideology which he has believed since the early 1950s, and in which a hardline view of the Cold War with the Soviet Union is very much central.

I would like to summarize some of the points of difference between this ideology or world view and that of the Nixon administration. It seems to me that they present a profound contrast. One point of comparison is that the Nixon administration accepted the notion of limits to U.S. power, and as a result accepted the need for an accommodation with the Soviet Union. Whatever the feeling after World War II about the United States being able to behave as an imperial power, by 1968–1969 there had been a recognition that the ballgame was different, that there were other centers of power and that some kind of détente, some kind of accommodation, had to be undertaken to establish new rules of the game—to establish limits, so that battles were not fought that were unnecessary and so that we would not blunder into the nuclear war that nobody wanted. The Reagan administration does not accept this idea of accommodation, of limits, and still thinks that we can return to the period right after World War II—not even the period of the missile crisis—the period right after World War II, when we had a nuclear monopoly, when the United States could pretty much call the shots.

Secondly, what seems to me another assumption that the Nixon administration came to accept was that the Soviet Union was not the center of all the problems in the world. Our current president has instead taken the view, as he told the *Wall Street Journal*, that there would not be hot spots in the world were it not for the Soviet Union. If we look at the Reagan speeches, there is a very simple line running through them that is at odds with the Nixon position, which is that all regional, racial, irrational, nationalistic, class sources of tension in the world are irrelevant. The only thing that is relevant is the East-West conflict. I do not think that was the view of the Nixon-Kissinger years. There was a recognition that the Arabs and Israelis, the black and white Africans, the juntas and the peasants in Central America, and so forth were fighting over things that might not necessarily be centered around Soviet foreign policy or Soviet expansionism. This administration does have that very simplistic view.

The third notion which the Nixon administration accepted was the belief that nuclear war was special—that there was a need for the superpowers to limit their areas of conflict to the diplomatic and the political realm, or, if necessary, to conventional wars, but that they had a common stake in avoiding nuclear war, and therefore in pursuing arms control. However cynical one may be about the progress that was made toward arms control, or even about the motivations of the superpowers, Nixon and the Soviets accepted the view that nuclear war put a special obligation on the superpowers. Arms control, détente, and everything that went with it was essential. It seems to me very clear by now that this administration is not interested in arms control, and sticks to the view, which it has stated many times, that there is no real inherent danger in the arms race—that you do not go to war by being too strong. When we look at very specific things that had been put in the arms control hopper by Nixon and pursued by the administrations since—the comprehensive test ban treaty, the anti-satellite weapons treaty, SALT II and III—these have now been abandoned. It is obvious that we have had a turning away from the previous view of nuclear war. Indeed, when we think of the President's "Star Wars" speech of March 23, 1983, where he talked about perhaps the most dangerous escalation of the arms race—the introduction of a whole new class of "third generation" nuclear weapons—this becomes even more apparent. It is a view of peace brought about not through arms control, not through the common working out of differences between the superpowers, but rather through technology, through an escalation of the arms race and through more weapons—peace at the end of *that* rainbow. That seems to be a rather serious departure from the consensus that had been developed under Nixon.

Finally, and most important in terms of the current ideological outlook as opposed to that of the Nixon administration, is the view that says that we are in the 1930s, that the Soviets are in the position of Hitler's Germany, that the Soviets feel that they can conquer, and want to conquer, the world in one way or another, either through blackmail or intimidation or actual fighting—and that, moreover, the existence of nuclear weapons does not profoundly alter their ambition. I think the Nixon administration had come to abandon such an analogy, and recognized that there were many things driving the Soviet Union—many forces, many concerns—and that there were bureaucratic problems in the Soviet Union, there were domestic economic problems, there were splits, there were different forces, different sources of power, etc. It was a much more complex view of the Soviet Union, and for that reason the analogy of the 1930s and of Hitler on the march did not hold. And even those who believed in the analogy thought that the existence of nuclear weapons would alter such expansionist dreams, and that the Soviets had come to recognize that. This administration, however, insists on the 1930s analogy, and I think that we are seriously underestimating this administration's ideological commitments. I think, moreover, that this constant reiteration of the 1930s analogy is terribly important.

Where did this ideology come from? If we look at the forces that came to power with the 1980 election, we find that they represent basically three components. First, you have the primitive anti-Soviet feeling of Ronald Reagan, Ed Meese, and those people. It has been around since the Bolshevik revolution. This approach could have become an isolationist, "fortress America" position, as it has in the past. But I suggest that because of a peculiar alliance with two other forces, it went the other way, and became very definitely internationalist, expansionist, and confrontationalist. The second element, which you have had for some time and which I think tends to be split on these questions right now, is what we used to refer to as the military-industrial complex, or the military-industrial-*intellectual* complex. Basically, to put it into its crudest form, these people have a stake in tension, and because they have a stake in tension—either an ego stake, a monetary stake, a career stake, or what have you—they tend to look at the evidence in a different way than an objective observer would look at the evidence. Much of our evaluation of the Soviet Union, of the Soviet threat, and the problems we have in the world comes from "think tanks"—not just at places like Rand and Livermore, but also at each of the big aerospace companies, which now have their own Soviet specialists. And much of the literature that has been turned out about our situation in the world and the dangers we face comes from these people who have a stake—whether they want to admit it or not—in a continuance of U.S.-Soviet tensions. And so the Nixon administration—to the degree that it moved away from the confrontationalist approach, to the degree that it embraced some sort of détente—would make these people uncomfortable, while Reagan's position would make them more content. But as I said before, there is a split in their ranks, having to do with the question of nuclear weapons. There are some people who have made their living in the military-industrial complex who have grandchildren that they care about, and summer homes that they care about, just as their Soviet counterparts do. And they draw the line at us getting too wild in our thinking about nuclear war. And so we have seen some very serious defections in the ranks. But, nonetheless, there is still a big powerful base of people who have a stake in confrontation, who have a stake in a Cold War, and who are inevitably aligned with people of a more primitive political perspective.

Then there is a third, and I think decisive, element in this new coalition, which is represented by the neoconservatives. I think it is the neoconservatives who made Reagan's view credible. I think it is neoconservatives who, consulting with Reagan and playing an absolutely decisive role in this administration, have provided the appearance at least of a more sophisticated analysis, with factual evidence and the like to package what would have been otherwise dismissed as an out-of-date ideology, an out-of-date approach. The neoconservatives have been particularly effective, beginning with their attacks on SALT II during the Carter administration, but coming to their fullest force with Reagan. What these people have been able to do, as I say, is to provide an intellectual aura for what really is basically a very primitive view of the world.

Finally, let me say something about the past, because the neoconservatives dwell on it. The main element in their analysis is that somehow we were deceived during the period of détente. We were deceived by the left, we were weakened internally, we were deceived by the Russians, and so forth. I think that this view is nonsense. I do not think we were deceived by the Russians. I do not think Richard Nixon was naive. The control of Soviet behavior through "linkage" to arms control negotiations was not accepted by the Nixon administration because they knew that you were mixing two separate issues—that if you accepted the idea that nuclear war was special, then you could not demand that kind of linkage. I would point out that the Soviets signed onto SALT I at a time when we were bombing their ally in North Vietnam—not only were we bombing their ally, but we bombed Haiphong when Kosygin was there—and this did not stop them from participating in these talks. They did not call off the talks, they did not say "the hell with détente" or with arms control; they pursued it. I think that the Nixon administration understood that. And all this current rewriting of history—this revisionism that says somehow, under the protection of détente, the Soviets were betraying the spirit of it and were doing something else—this denies the whole basis of détente.

Secondly, I think there has been a great deal of distortion of factual evidence to show that the Soviets have engaged in an unwarranted and unprecedented arms build-up. I am not going to defend the Soviet build-up. I am not going to defend either of the superpowers' build-ups. But in my book *With Enough Shovels*, I have a quote from Robert McNamara that I think is quite revealing on this point. McNamara says had he been his Soviet counterpart when he was the U.S. secretary of defense, he would have launched precisely the same build-up the Soviets have engaged in these last twenty years. That was Robert McNamara. And I think we have had ample testimony from people who ran this country's national security and defense policy for the last twenty-five years that, in fact, we are not Number 2, that this is a red herring. We recently had a leaked CIA report that said that we had exaggerated the Soviet build-up by a factor of 100 percent. Instead of an increase of 4 percent a year, they have been increasing 2 percent a year, which was roughly under their Gross National Product. In my book, I document the "Team B" effort to distort the reporting of the CIA, but I think basically we have been subjected to an enormous fear campaign by the neoconservatives about the Soviet build-up, exaggerating it, throwing it out of proportion, in an attempt to discredit the policy of détente and arms control. We have also had a great fear campaign launched about Soviet success, suggesting that somehow the Soviets are doing terribly well. I do not think I have to elaborate on this point, but it seems to me that just a cursory examination of the past twenty-five years will show not only that the Soviets have not done very well, but that neither superpower has really improved its position in proportion to its increase in nuclear or conventional military power. The Soviets clearly did better as a world power before they had the atomic bomb. They did better in the 1950s than in the 1960s. They did better in the 1960s then in the 1970s. We can talk about China, we can talk about Egypt, etc. But that chart that Casey and Reagan put on the wall about great Soviet successes is just not supported by the evidence, and people must know that.

Finally, I want to say that I do not accept the mood of doom and gloom that I have heard at conferences of this sort. I do not think that it is so easy to slip back into the 1950s. I think we live in a very, very different society. Let me just briefly say why. First, the international situation is so obviously different that it is very difficult for the administration to support its position. There *has* been a Sino-Soviet dispute, and the argument by the New Left in the 1960s about Communism being able to be nationalist has been amply confirmed by the dispute between Vietnam and China. So the attempt to turn back the clock to the point where we have an "international Communist conspiracy," with a timetable for its takeover of the world, just does not work. There is just too much evidence that keeps popping up that denies it. And there are too many movements that occur in the world which oppose us or oppose the Russians and do not fit into that simple view. So the grand theory of this administration keeps running into trouble.

Secondly, there are different forces now than in the 1950s. In the 1950s, the Catholic church was the most solid base of support for the Cold War—if you recall Cardinal Spellman and Cardinal MacIntyre, and so forth. At this point, the Catholic church is playing, it seems to me, a leading role in challenging this simplistic thinking about the Cold War and certainly about nuclear weapons. But there are many other forces, and basically I think that, whereas in the 1960s the opposition to the Vietnam war almost had to assume the trappings of a counterculture movement, of a counter-establishment movement, what we are seeing now is very much a movement from the mainstream of America. It is very much a movement of the center trying to regroup. It is very much a middle-class movement, especially when you talk about the Physicians for Social Responsibility—which I think is one of the most important grass-roots movements in a long time—or you talk about the Catholic church, or you talk about William Colby who had supported the Operation Phoenix program in Vietnam and who now supports the Nuclear Freeze, or you talk about Robert McNamara or McGeorge Bundy—who we used to think of as Dr. Strangelove in the 1960s. If you look at the people who are really leading the opposition to this trend to a more dangerous Cold War, they are former leaders of the Center. And to my mind, that is a source of optimism. I would not say blind optimism, because these people are also capable of being chicken, and they are capable of getting confused very easily. But it is a source of optimism nonetheless.

# EDWARD P. THOMPSON

Historian;
founder, European Nuclear Disarmament (END)

## The Ideology of Exterminism

[. . .] There is a sense in which the Cold War is now about nothing but itself.

It is there because it is there because it is there. And because interests have become obstructions and inertias, and because it is, in fact, more unpleasant and more difficult to move out of these received habits and inertias than to effect the rather dramatic and, from the standpoint of establishments—East and West—possibly destabilizing effects of moving beyond those parameters altogether. The political and military leaders are acted upon by the Cold War, rather than being actors. This is clearly true in the West, but also in the East, sometimes in more reactive ways. On both sides political leaders are simply being carried along by this inertial thrust. One of the first things that the international peace movement is about is to make such a clatter and disturbance that it becomes more painful for them to go on as they are than to change, to make it more difficult for them to continue in the ways they are going.

One example of the Cold War being about itself is what we could call "technology creep." The laboratories exist, and since they exist they are continually developing sweet new technologies. When they have invented these technologies, they have to find some way of placing them and therefore they have to invent situations in which they are needed. So some of the military and political arguments for the existence of these weapons are thought up *after* the weapons have already been invented. On both sides of the Atlantic, even in the peace movement, people have been indoctrinated with the argument that SS20s on one side, and Cruise and

36

Pershings on the other, are answers to each other. Many people are not aware of the fact that these two weapons systems were developed totally independently of each other. It was only after they were developed that they became part of the military-political game.

I am even more concerned with the ideological and political creep of the Cold War than I am with technology creep. The Cold War can be seen as a process which has acquired its own interests, so that important ruling sectors in society actually need its continuance—not only to justify their huge appropriations of the taxes, the resources, and the skills of their own societies, but as a means of internal social control and internal intellectual control. It is always useful to have the threat of the enemy as a means of bringing internal dissent into line. For both sides this is effective internally and as a means of control of client states. The notion of an enemy threat affords a justification for maintaining subordinate states in a position of cliency. This sense of external threat has become part of the very identity of many citizens of the United States and the Soviet Union. The citizens of the Soviet Union feel themselves to be inheritors of a revolution threatened by the imperialist and capitalist West. Soviet children learn in school that being Soviet citizens requires resistance to a threatening capitalist West. In the United States, which was created out of wave after wave of immigration, there has been a similar process of the creation of national identity out of opposition to the other. First it was anti-anarchism, anti-socialism, and then anti-communism which became part of the ideological cement that stuck together the notion of what it was to be a free American.

In Eastern and Western Europe, both of which are made up of client states, subjected to the hegemony of their own superpowers, this kind of ideological cohesion does not work so well. Increasing numbers of Eastern and Western Europeans find themselves in a no-man's land. If there has to be a nuclear war, it would be much more convenient for the superpowers to use Europe as a battlefield than to actually strike at each other's cities. Many Europeans find a common interest in resistance to the born-again Christians and the stillborn Marxists on the other side who are arguing above their heads.

This ideological and political creep is even more dangerous than weapons creep. In fact, it carries the weapons creep forward. It is the adversary posture of the two blocs that is the ultimate derangement of human civilization, out of which new weapons systems continually arise. Look at the papers: MX one week, nerve gas, B1 bomber. These weapons systems seem to be arising one after another, both through their own thrust and because of the posture of the blocs. We are now in the last phase in which a reversal is possible. The peace consciousness that has arisen now will not stay around forever. I believe we have about five years to reverse this process. If we fail in the next five years, I do not think the next generation will have another chance.

This inertial thrust toward confrontation also provides an apologia for interventionism by one superpower or another. It is used to excuse Soviet actions in Afghanistan. Cold War apologetics are used to justify United States intervention in Central America. Special hawkish interests take advantage of this confrontational situation for their own purposes.

There is an element of sheer contingency and accident in all this. Between 1945 and 1948, there was a global political-ideological confrontation whose epicenter was in Europe. It was simply accidental that nuclear technology, the technology of mass extermination, was invented at the same time, in 1945, and its efficacy was demonstrated beyond all shadow of a doubt at Hiroshima and Nagasaki. These two things came together not by any plan, but by accident. This mutual nuclear threat has arrested all other political and diplomatic processes for the normal resolution of differences. From the moment that this arbitrary line, the Yalta line, was drawn across Europe, and a rather more complicated line was drawn across Asia, there has been a true freeze. All the normal channels and currents of cultural and political communication between East and West have turned to ice. For thirty-five years the balance of terror has held rigid. The initial confrontation has been protracted long after the moment of its origin. The Cold Warriors offer to extend it everlastingly into the future. One of the extraordinary things about the war movement—those who call themselves the "defense community"—is that they have marvelously sophisticated arguments about balance and control and verification. But if you ask them, "When does it end? When do you see the Cold War ending? By what means?" they have no answer. No answer at all. They have no political resolution to offer.

So the nuclear confrontation is in essence a substitution of the technology of extermination for a political resolution. The international peace movement is, by the same argument, really a movement for a human thaw, for a process by which these glaciers that have arrested human communication will thaw once more and the rivers of communication will run and find new channels. And if you freeze any bioprocess—and politics is a bioprocess—I believe it is true that ultimately degeneration of the tissues begins to set in. This is why I think our condition is terminal. The arrest, the stasis of democratic process and communication process, has led to the arrest or the reversal of normal internal processes within both blocs themselves [. . .]

What frightens me is the very high degree of ideology in this renewed Cold War, and the very low degree of genuine interests at stake. The actual conflict of interest between the adversary blocs is really very low, at least on the European continent. Half of the so-called peoples' democracies in Eastern Europe are in hock to Western bankers. There is an increasing flow of trade between East and West. Whenever the Cold War dies down, there is an increasing flow of ideas and communication. You go to Budapest and no important book published here—in New York, Berlin, Paris, London—is not on someone's shelf in Budapest within twelve months. You go to Prague and you find people wearing the same gear as they are wearing in London or San Francisco, and you find that they are playing the same pop music on their transistor radios. The reality is that the successor generations particularly are beginning to abandon the postures and adversary positions of the Cold War. But the military and political establishments, the old elite, are terrified of the instability that this might result in, and are actually reinforcing and holding the divided world in place. They are falling back onto reflexes inherited from the first Cold War. This is what Mrs. Thatcher is doing with her imitation of Churchill; this is what President Reagan is doing when he speaks of the Soviet Union as an evil empire. This presentation of the superpowers as polar opposites is an ideological imposition, but an ideology armed with the most devastating instruments of death [. . .]

# MARTIN J. SHERWIN

Professor of History, Tufts University

# The Sources of American Conduct

I have been asked to speak on the topic of "A Historical Perspective on the First and Second Cold War," an interesting task, but alas, one that I am unable to perform. I am not convinced that the first Cold War ever ended.

We have had warmer and colder periods in our relations with the Soviet Union. Détente was the warmest. But in the aftermath, especially with the election of Ronald Reagan, relations with the Soviet Union chilled.

But what, I have asked proponents of the "New Cold War" theory, is "fundamentally new" about the Reagan administration's policies? The most frequent answers consider Reagan's concept of a protracted conflict, his hostility to détente, and his general aping of the attitudes of the Truman administration.

On the last point I rest my case. There has been *one* Cold War punctuated by a period of a more civilized and peaceful relationship—détente. But the principles upon which the entire Cold War has rested—from the U.S. side at least—are principles that were set in place during the Truman years. Though submerged, these principles continued to operate during détente, which explains how they were so easily salvaged by President Reagan.

If we are ever going to find policies that might lead away from the Cold War, we must understand the foundations upon which our foreign policies rest.

World War II ended almost forty years ago, but we continue to build on its ashes. The "lessons" of history that have shaped U.S. policymaking since 1945 are the lessons we have culled from the wreckage of that devastating war.

It is understandable, indeed it is right, that we learn from those terrible years. In 1945 "never again" echoed as clearly through the corridors of power in Washington, Moscow, and London as it did through the streets of Palestine.

And what did we learn about preventing war from World War II?

The most deeply felt lesson was that appeasement stimulates the appetite of an aggressor. This lesson lies at the foundation of the Cold War, and it is a lesson as deeply felt by the Soviets as by the statesmen who manage the diplomacy of Western nations.

Appeasement phobia lies at the foundation of our containment policy. It has been a consistent theme in U.S. diplomacy since 1945, and no serious alternatives to the Cold War will be possible until our political culture rids itself of this political neurosis. I call it a phobia because it is an emotional commitment, and because it does us great harm. Appeasement phobia undermines peace. It sees our relations with the Soviet Union as a zero-sum game. It implies that any negotiation that does not result in clear advantages for the United States has resulted in dangerous advantages for the Soviet Union. In effect, it rejects diplomacy, the process of bargaining and compromise. And it rejects the concept of mutual advantage—a necessary frame of reference for survival in the nuclear age.

The same fear of appeasement keeps U.S. politics resolutely anti-Soviet. To label a politician "soft on Communism" is, in effect, to identify him as one who would willingly pursue the bankrupt diplomacy of the 1930s. U.S. politicians would rather drown than carry an umbrella home from a Soviet-American negotiating session.

The second "lesson" that comes out of World War II is the lesson of Pearl Harbor. On December 7, 1941, Americans learned the consequences of not being prepared. Preparedness became another postwar theme. Next time we had to be ready. At first, the time frame was weeks, then it was days, later it became hours, and now it is minutes. The quivering finger held over the nuclear button has become the symbol of our age.

The third "lesson" that has been consistently accepted since World War II is that United States isolationism leads to world chaos. We may not want to be the world's policeman, but we have no choice. Without our leadership and power either Europe will drift into the arms of the East, or war will envelop it. In either case, we lose.

All of these "lessons" are part of the foundation of the Cold War, for we have applied them against the Soviet Union as we learned them from Germany and Japan. Until they are unlearned, reformulated, or seriously modified, until our political culture rejects the analogy between Nazi Germany and Soviet Russia, the Cold War will be with us—the genuine, original version set in place during the Truman administration will be with us.

The U.S. government's political use of nuclear weapons has played a major role in supporting that Cold War. The development and use of those nuclear weapons, and the concomitant understanding of their destructive power, did not alter the behavior of nation states, of the United States and the Soviet Union in particular. It merely added a dimension of unprecedented horror to the risk of war.

Nevertheless, since 1945, both sides have recklessly approached the nuclear brink: the Berlin blockade of 1948, the Berlin crisis of 1961, the Cuban missile crisis of 1962, the 1973 nuclear alert are a few examples offering proof that the diplomatic game of threat and counterthreat has not been eliminated by the development of weapons that could destroy the world. Indeed, the history of U.S.–Soviet relations during the Cold War makes a strong case for Einstein's aphorism (in slightly modified form) that with the development of the atomic bomb, "everything changed except the way we think" (and I would add, speak).

The superpower dialogue has been infused with apocalyptic awareness, but that has not prevented nuclear weapons from being integrated into the everyday business of diplomacy, as Daniel Ellsberg has demonstrated in his article "A Call to Mutiny" (in Dan Smith and E. P. Thompson's *Protest and Survive* [New York: Monthly Review Press, 1981]). From Truman to Reagan, every administration has employed the threat of nuclear war either to gain political advantage, or to prevent a Soviet initiative.

Behind these nuclear threats lies a strategy, grounded in the "lessons" of World War II, that has locked U.S. Cold War policies into an anti-Soviet matrix from which it cannot escape. That matrix is based on three objectives that were set in place during the Truman years, and that have been consistently maintained to the present, even through the period of détente. Taken together, they define our major Cold War objectives: (1) to keep the Soviets from expanding their borders; (2) to keep Communism out of the industrialized world; (3) to keep Communism out of the third world. These objectives have been the foundation of our foreign policy: during the Truman administration, during the Reagan administration, and during all administrations in between—including those that embraced détente. To understand how the Cold War is managed from Washington, it is necessary to examine these objectives.

The strategy for achieving the first objective—to keep the Soviet Union from expanding its borders—was secretly sketched out for the department of state by George Kennan in his famous long telegram of February 1946, and repeated for the public in his well-known "Mr. X" article in *Foreign Affairs* of July 1947. Once accepted, the containment doctrine evolved into economic support, through the Truman Doctrine and the Marshall Plan, then into a traditional military alliance bolstered by conventional forces, and, finally, into a nuclear armed alliance that threatened nuclear war in order to keep the Soviet Union at bay.

The strategy for achieving the second objective—to keep Communism out of the industrialized world, especially Western Europe—followed the same pattern. The United States' economic reconstruction of Western Europe was tied to the formation of the European Defense Community. Then nuclear weapons, by contributing to the political stability of the alliance system, became tied to domestic political issues. By the early 1950s, nuclear weapons were politicized, providing a symbolic military-political link between the defense of Western Europe and the defense of North America.

By the early 1960s the strategies for achieving these two objectives had been accepted. The Kennedy years were a time of testing for the Soviet Union, but the managers of U.S. foreign policy held fast to the principles they had inherited. The world survived the

Berlin crisis of 1961 and the Cuban missile crisis of 1962. Thereafter, the belief was politically unshakable that nuclear deterrence could both contain the Soviet Union and prevent nuclear war.

But a successful strategy for achieving the third objective—keeping Communism out of the third world—continued to elude American planners. Neither Special Forces nor an army of half a million worked in Vietnam.

The Reagan administration's nuclear weapons policies (which include its calculated, cavalier rhetoric about U.S. plans for fighting a nuclear war are part of its effort to solve this final conundrum facing U.S. foreign policy. Its approach begins with a simple question: if nuclear weapons have managed to keep the Soviet Union out of Western Europe, and if they have aided in keeping Communism out of the industrialized world, why could they not also contribute to keeping Communism out of the third world?

The Reaganuts believed they could, and the administration came into office with a strategy to do it. They would leave the Soviet Union with a simple choice. First, they could try to keep up with us in the nuclear arms race, and pay the economic consequences of their folly. The harm that such a decision would inflict on the Soviet economy would be a victory of sorts for the United States. Or, they could choose not to keep up with us; in that case they would face the possibility of another humiliation like the Cuban missile crisis. This would also be perceived as a victory, since the concept of nuclear blackmail is an article of faith among Reagan administration strategists. Finally, the Soviet Union could choose to come to nuclear arms negotiations ready to accept the connection we seek between arms control and foreign policy in general. In other words, they could agree to withdraw support for wars of national liberation in exchange for a nuclear weapons agreement.

The problems with such a U.S. strategy are obvious to many outside the administration. First, it has not worked and it will not work. And, second, it increases the danger of nuclear war, a danger that cannot be responsibly ignored.

George Kennan, whose eloquence galvanized the anti-Soviet forces within the government in 1946, has, ironically, helped to galvanize the anti-nuclear forces outside the government in the 1980s. His fundamental point: there is no issue between the

United States and the Soviet Union, absolutely nothing, that can possibly be worth a nuclear war. Until that point is understood, accepted, and acted upon, the Cold War, as it was fashioned during the Truman administration, will be with us.

*In the discussion following the panel presentations, the following question was asked from the audience: Can you really distinguish between the Cold War and the U.S.-Soviet rivalry? If it is not possible, it seems to me, the outcome is only disaster.*

*Sherwin:* I do not think that the Cold War can be distinguished from the U.S.-Soviet rivalry: by definition that rivalry *is* the Cold War. But at the same time I do not believe that our rivalry must necessarily result in disaster. On the contrary, it is my point that to avoid disaster we must understand, publicly expose, and eliminate the *irrational* sources of our hostility. We must realize that too often we are trapped by our rhetoric, by our economic totems, by our political culture, and by our historical "lessons." We are trapped within this Cold War system, which is global, which is dynamic, which encompasses everything including the way we think. We have to start the process of escaping from our Cold War mindset. For example, it is clear to me that our most important current alliance is not the NATO alliance, as we are told by our government and the press. *Our most important alliance is our alliance with the Soviet Union to prevent a nuclear war.* When you think of the U.S.-Soviet nuclear relationship in alliance terms, you recognize that there has to be a restructuring of our thinking. If a presidential candidate had the courage to say on national television that the most important alliance in the world is the alliance between the United States and the Soviet Union, then the public would begin the process of rethinking its Cold War assumptions. That would help to mitigate the danger of a disaster.

# GEORGE W. BRESLAUER

Professor of Political Science, University of California, Berkeley

# The Global Dynamics of Cold War

The current international situation is one of two global superpowers competing for influence and allies in areas that are not vital to their national security concerns. This global competition is not my definition of Cold War. When people speak about the Cold War they often speak past each other, partly because they use very different definitions of the term. A U.S. invasion of Nicaragua, despicable as it would be, would not necessarily be a Cold War act, because it does not threaten the Soviet Union directly. Since global competition existed even during the height of détente, I would distinguish between détente and Cold War, rather than seeing détente merely as another form of Cold War. By détente I mean a situation where global competition is accompanied and tempered, but not eliminated, by sustained efforts to negotiate compromises in many issue areas, including, at a minimum, the arms race. I would refer to détente as collaborative competition. I would call the Cold War confrontational competition. Cold War (or confrontational) competition is competition that is accompanied and partially exacerbated by an arms race, rhetorical acrimony, military threats, and lack of progress in the area of collaborative negotiation.

In the current global competition in which the Soviet Union and the United States are engaged, what are the factors that are predominant and fuel the competition? The first is that great powers, after being locked for decades in competition, typically do not opt out of it unless the other side does so simultaneously. So the best prediction, even if it is a gloomy prediction, is that the current competition is a given and will continue. Second, numerous conflicts of interest do and will exist between the Soviet Union and the United States, although they will not necessarily be conflicts of economic interest. Third, in this global dynamic there is a very fuzzy line between the offense and the defense, between ambition and fear. I think Ralph K. White titled his recent book nicely, because his title neatly captured this mixture of offensive and defensive consideration on both sides. He referred to the Soviet Union and the United States as "Fearful Warriors." In some situations it may be easy to define whether one power is on the offensive or on the defensive, but in most situations it is not, because they typically view themselves as acting self-righteously in self-defense. Fourth, both sides, after decades of Cold War, have military-industrial complexes supported by civilian zealots with a wide range of political beliefs who happen to agree on bureaucratic, military, economic, or ideological predispositions to worst-case assumptions about the other superpower. What is most frustrating about worst-case assumptions in the current situation is that they are not in most instances falsifiable.

In this bipolar world we live in, with its legacy of hostility and mistrust, confrontational competition or Cold War is a higher probability than collaborative competition or détente. But this is a probability statement, not a certainty statement, because some things are not givens in this relationship. The scope of competition is not given; neither is the intensity nor the objects of competition. How a given leadership or administration on either side chooses to define vital interests that need to be defended is also not a given. Regardless of who is in power, the Soviet Union will always choose Eastern Europe as a vital interest, and the United States sees Western Europe as such. But for those gray areas that constitute most of the world, the definition of vital interests worth fighting for is a variable that can change depending upon the politics of the moment. A fifth variable that is not a given is the degree of inclination on either side, at any point in time, to use its military forces—or the threat or use of its military forces—to compel the other side to back down. Similarly, the degree of inclination for collaboration on each side is not a given. So all of these may vary depending upon political pressures both from within the political establishment and from without, and depending upon the lessons drawn by given leaders from prior experience.

Looked at in these terms, what are the incentives in the next five to ten years for tempering the competitive givens between the United States and the Soviet Union such that collaborative competition will be more probable than confrontational competition? I would point to five such incentives. The first is the fear of nuclear war, whether by crisis escalation or by accident. While this fear has been with us for decades, we now are reaching a point of public mobilization and awareness of the implications of new weapons systems, in both the United States and Western Europe, that has intensified the fear of nuclear war on both sides. This becomes an incentive for tempering the competition. Second, there is a more heightened awareness than earlier of the inherently uncontrollable nature of the third world. Both the Soviet Union and the United States have learned this lesson the hard way. That does not mean they have opted out of attempting to consolidate gains in the third world, but it does mean they have become much more selective in their targets, going more for easier wins than for tougher ones. Third, there is an increased awareness of the economic and political costs of the arms race. In the Soviet Union the awareness is more of the economic costs; in the United States the awareness of the economic costs apparently has not yet sunk in and the fears are more based upon political anxieties.

A fourth incentive for tempering the competition is an increased awareness on both sides of either the economic costs or the inefficiency—that is to say, the lack of a lasting payoff—that comes from a heavy investment in competition in distant areas. Neither global containment nor global counter-containment is going to be feasible or economically bearable. And finally there is a more selective definition on both sides of what's worth defending, resulting in caution in the commitment of armed forces in turbulent areas of relatively low interest.

The most optimistic scenario for the next ten years that I can muster, given my belief that competition will continue and only its degree is in question, is a vision of a combination of selective containment, counter-containment, and selective collaboration or détente. I can see agreement in limited areas to head off worst-case possibilities for both sides. That will imply a certain measure of mutual avoidance where the two superpowers in effect temper the competition without formal agreements. An example of this is Afghanistan, where the United States did not respond in any escalatory manner on the ground there. The pessimistic scenario revolves around an arms race that raises the probability of an accidental nuclear war, crisis escalation in hot spots as a result of superpower acrimony, and/or minimalist agreements that do not really harness any of the components of the competition that have high potential for escalation. I will not venture a prediction as to which scenario is the more likely to be realized.

. . .

[. . .] One view of the growth of Soviet military power is that Soviet military procurement decisions are entirely internally generated. They are products of a combination of civilian zealotry and the power of the military-industrial complex in Soviet politics. And that what we have been watching for the last twenty or thirty years is an inexorable build-up that was destined to occur, and that we have finally realized was going on. That is one view.

Another view that I find more satisfying as a historian of this period is that, while the military-industrial complex was a very powerful actor in Soviet politics, and while party zealots who are also powerful actors have had a predisposition toward viewing military power as the only guarantee of their security in the world, there have been and continue to be key turning points in the development of Soviet politics when there is greater openness or space for political innovation, when there is a demonstrated inclination to innovate in the direction of holding down the rate of growth of military expenditures and making certain types of concessions in order to harness the arms race. And the reason that I think these historical points of reference are relevant is because I believe that we are at another such historical turning point now. If the current situation continues unchanged, my prediction would be that we will live to regret it.

After Stalin's death, the Soviet leadership realized that it was in a particularly ticklish situation internationally. The Korean war was still going on, but the opening began. There was substantial consensus—not total consensus, but substantial consensus—in the Soviet leadership at the time about the desirability and necessity of such an opening to the West, but considerable conflict over what the terms of that opening should be. Some people argued that we need to engage in a defense build-up so that we have bargaining chips with which to deal with the United States and Western Europe; others argued that we now have enough military might and that we should go directly into arms control negotiations and negotiate quite seriously. There is considerable evidence to suggest that those who were arguing that the Soviet Union had enough already were thrown onto the political defensive in 1954—and the timing of these signs coincides extraordinarily with two things going on in the West: one, the heavy emphasis under John Foster Dulles on massive retaliation and rollback of Communism, and two, the whole issue of German rearmament, which was on the agenda of the Western powers. You can trace the debates between Khrushchev, who in this debate was the hardliner, and Malenkov, who was calling for moderation in defense expenditures because he had other priorities at the time that he wanted to pump. And you can see Malenkov going on the defensive with each repetition of the Western threats regarding German rearmament or regarding the rollback of Communism.

The next turning point where you can observe a similar phenomenon comes in 1960–61, with the collapse of the efforts of 1959 toward some sort of U.S.–Soviet rapprochement. After the collapse of the Paris Summit in spring of 1960, you find Khrushchev, who in the previous year had been flirting with the idea of trying to strike some sort of deal to harness the arms race on the basis of present levels (rather than on the basis of what he had been arguing six years earlier, that we have to build up in the Soviet Union before we can face the United States so we will have bargaining chips) going on the defensive. And you find him going on the defensive ever more fully after Kennedy goes to Congress in his first month of power with a budget that calls for a 30 percent increase in U.S. military spending. It is from this point that you can date the huge Soviet commitment to the research, development, production, and deployment of the missile force that we saw come on line in the 1970s. The Soviets *did* launch a huge military build-up in the early 1960s, and you can see components of it being closely affected in their timing by the timing of the Kennedy build-up. But it was not an across-the-board build-up, and you can find Khrushchev in 1963 and 1964 still trying to hold the line, still in favor of strategic build-up but arguing that "we've got to draw the line on expenditures and hold down a conventional build-up." In fact, the evidence is not just suggestive, but overwhelming that Khrushchev's attacks on military spending at this time were virtually scuttling the Soviet program for fighter-bomber development—a program that does not get revived until after Khrushchev is out of power.

And, indeed, there is evidence that after Khrushchev is out of power you have another political succession during which the regime has multiple needs and multiple priorities, has a substantial consensus that it has to maintain military parity, that it has to be a global power, that it has to compete with the United States for influence and allies, but does *not* have agreement on how much it has to spend in order to defend or advance its interests. There is a debate going on at this time, and it is clear that the turning point in that debate comes in the summer or late spring of 1965, when those who were arguing that we have enough or that we do not have to accelerate current rates of military spending get thrown on the defensive. And that is after Lyndon Johnson adopts Barry Goldwater's policies toward Vietnam and the Americanization of the Vietnam war, with immense uncertainty as to whether it will escalate or not. And what happens at this point is that the Soviets then decide on the approach they are going to take to the arms race, which is an across-the-board pumping of all sectors of the defense establishment. It is at this point that those things in the conventional area, such as the fighter-bomber industry, get revived and get pumped up in a massive way. And those are the things that we start seeing coming on line in the 1970s.

Well, two of the three examples I have given you are examples from periods of obvious political succession, and the middle example that I gave you was from a period when Khrushchev was on the political defensive because his policies were failing. In other words, in all cases authority is precarious. And what we have in the

Soviet Union today is a repeat of history—a period when there are crying needs for alternative uses of funds, when authority is precarious because of a political succession, and when the United States is in a process of build-up and remilitarization in the belief, mistaken or otherwise, that that is the only thing the Soviets will listen to, that when you develop your bargaining chips the Soviets will cave in at negotiations. In fact, I think the historical evidence suggests quite the opposite—that the Soviet hardliners win in that kind of political atmosphere.

# LEON WOFSY

Professor of Immunology, Emeritus,
University of California, Berkeley

# Can the Cold War Be Ended?

Sonic booms from U.S. overflights of Managua and Corinto saluted Ronald Reagan's reelection. This is not an easy time for taking the long view, for offering a perspective on the "Cold War and beyond."

Nevertheless, we can contribute something to the motivation and energy for peace if we can begin to establish that a noncatastrophic end to the Cold War is actually a possibility for our time.

There is no lack of wishing and of exhortation. But there has been little analysis on which to base hopes for a peaceful ending. What discourages positive thinking is the sense that the Cold War is rooted in the very nature of the contending societies. That is a perception shared in different ways by those who vigorously pursue the Cold War and by many opponents of the arms race.

The question is: Can the United States and the Soviet Union, as both societies now exist, give up the Cold War?

I would like to consider the proposition that what some have called the "Second Cold War" may prove to be the last. This is not a novel notion if taken to mean that Cold War could end in hot war, in nuclear annihilation. Rather I want to look at the less obvious prospect, that the fifteen years remaining to the twentieth century could bring a historic break away from the Cold War, a significant movement toward a safer world.

That possibility does not rest on a prediction that either U.S. or Soviet society will undergo any fundamental transformation in the next generation, or that the inherent rivalry of basically differing societies is coming to an end. It depends on an estimate that the world has changed in ways that doom the Cold War to failure, that make it both more dangerous and more futile and difficult to sustain.

53

Peaceful termination of the Cold War phase of U.S.-Soviet competition requires that both powers make a genuine mutual commitment to prevent both nuclear war and conventional wars that could trigger catastrophe. That, of course, means stopping the arms race and reducing arms levels drastically—eventually enough to defang superpower rivalry of the instant capacity for world annihilation.

As sensible as that may be, we can hardly expect it unless we can reasonably make some other assessments about our changing world. The Cold War will not be discarded until the interests and purposes it serves are clearly outweighed by its failures. It will not end unless the United States and the Soviet Union can accept as irreversible fact the inability of either side to win victory over the other, in cold war or hot.

What changes bring into question whether the Cold War can remain, on balance, "functional"?

A hallmark of the Cold War has been the subordination of virtually every international and domestic issue to the U.S.-Soviet antagonism, engulfing especially every third world conflict and problem. However, one can argue that the capacity of the U.S.-Soviet rivalry to dominate the international scene is diminishing. Restrictions are increasing on the ability of either superpower to determine the actions of other nations and to control developments in the third world.

A huge contradiction has become evident in today's world: there is a remarkable gap between military power and its effective expression as political power. While military might now exceeds anything it was possible even to conceive of not long ago, there are also unprecedented barriers to the use of that force to impose ultimatums or win wars.

In a recent lecture at the University of California at Berkeley, Seweryn Bialer talked about the difficulty of perceiving long-term changes while they are happening. To get a sense of the direction of events, it is worth making some comparisons between the world of the first Cold War (beginning in the late 1940s) and that of the second (beginning a little over thirty years later).

After World War II, the powerful United States and the war-devastated Soviet Union each had its own aspirations to world leadership. The United States moved into a most ambitious role in the postwar world. Based on a dominance of world power that was without precedent in modern history, it exercised authority over weaker capitalist states and assumed interests the latter could not maintain. It took on the mission of turning back Communist influence in Europe and of checking a worldwide spread of anti-imperialist revolutions. The Soviet Union made its first priority the attempt to guarantee that Europe, especially Germany, could never again be mobilized for the destruction of the Soviet Union. It also saw a historic opportunity in the postwar collapse of the colonial empires and the rising popular support for socialism. It viewed itself at the head of an ascendant socialist and third world camp, one that could ultimately surpass the United States as the dominant international influence.

After a brief and limited respite in the 1970s, the second Cold War began in conditions of enormous growth of military power on both sides, each having achieved the capacity for the extinction of life on earth. But neither side has gained overriding nuclear or space supremacy.

Both sides have had to countenance major setbacks: for the United States, the failure to win costly wars in Korea and Vietnam, the inability to pacify the third world and to prevent revolutions even in the Central American "backyard," the pressure of rising economic challenges from Japan and Europe, and the escalating burden of national debt; for the Soviet Union, collapse of the China alliance, significant failures in the third world, an inability to gain popular support and prevent unrest in Eastern Europe, chronic economic shortcomings at home, and a protracted war in Afghanistan.

Guerrilla wars, revolutions, national and religious uprisings have occurred in many parts of the third world. Wars of intervention, however, have often failed to achieve their objectives and, from a political standpoint, have become more difficult to mount. Against glorified military ventures in little Grenada and the Falklands, one must weigh the mixed results and frustrations of wars in Vietnam, Lebanon, and Afghanistan.

The obstacles that doom any superpower bid for world supremacy go well beyond fear of the other superpower. That is seen best in the third world, where patterns of turmoil cannot be accommodated to the interests of old- or new-style colonial control. The "zero-sum" game breaks down badly in the third world—a defeat for U.S. interests in Iran does not put the Soviet Union in the driver's seat; nor does the exclusion of the Soviet Union from the negotiating process in the Middle East make possible a Pax Americana for that region.

Even though détente in the 1970s did not end the arms race or prevent resumption of the "new" Cold War, it reflected the beginning of a reluctant adjustment to growing limitations on superpower expectations. Within the United States, cracks appeared in some of the pillars of popular faith in a Cold War view of the world: the "Vietnam syndrome" replaced a belief in U.S. invincibility with opposition to new military adventures; the myth of a monolithic Communist enemy under Soviet control was a less acceptable explanation for every challenge in the third world; there was growing recognition that neither side can win the superpower contest, that survival makes the need for some accommodation inescapable.

Unfortunately, changing world realities have not yielded automatic acceptance, universal sanity. Factors that drive the Cold War on toward disaster remain a large part of present reality. They, too, have to figure strongly in our estimate of the extent to which the United States and the Soviet Union can or will accommodate to the constraints each confronts.

Although détente was discarded before Ronald Reagan's first term, he quickly made the new Cold War his own. Reagan brought America back—back to old crusades and to delusions that had begun to break down under the strain of Vietnam.

How, so soon after Reagan's landslide election, is it possible to foresee a turn away from the Cold War over the next fifteen years?

Bizarre as the notion might seem, it may be that a historic paradox attaches to the Reagan presidency. His very effort to gain a decisive victory in the Cold War and the arms race, to quell all the "hot spots" in the third world, may evoke the evidence and the response that finally compel a change of course. If the most militant and militaristic Cold Warrior of all cannot overcome the windmills of reality, who will be able to do so after him?

I do not think that Reagan entered his second administration with intentions that depart significantly from those he brought with him into the White House. The second four years are bound to hold even greater dangers than the first four. While the President and his men have shown flexibility in adjusting the game plan, there is no doubt that they are playing to win. They may talk with the Soviets, even seek some expedient deals, but they have no thought of relaxing the relentless pressure of the military build-up. They expect to expand covert interventionist activity aimed at provoking and exploiting fissures in the Soviet system. They will tolerate no Marxist government or revolutionary movement in the Western hemisphere. Clearly they intend to knock out Nicaragua and subdue Central America one way or another, and they will look for any opportunity to move against Cuba. The Cold War will continue to serve as the rationale for military alliances with extreme reactionary regimes around the world.

Yet there can be a large distance between intentions and capacity. This was evident in the first Reagan administration: its successes were major, but so were its failures.

It succeeded in spearheading political gains for the right not only at home, but in Europe. It aroused a spirit of "born-again" Americanism, which measures patriotism in equal parts of flag waving, militarism, and religious fundamentalism. It got its way with everything it demanded for unlimited arms expansion and for the deployment of Pershing and Cruise missiles in Europe. In so doing, it gave accelerated momentum to basic drives that will be the greatest obstacle to curbing the arms race and ending the Cold War in the years ahead.

However, the Reagan administration, especially in its first three years, also managed to frighten the world, including Americans, as never before about the extreme danger of nuclear war. The recklessness of intensified Cold War, epitomized by Reagan's own conduct and rhetoric, evoked alarm even among proponents of earlier Cold War policies. Despite Reagan's escape from the potential consequences of the Lebanon disaster, he showed that there was no taste among most Americans for high-risk military adventures. Early in the 1984 election year, it was deemed necessary to subdue the style of the supreme Cold Warrior and elevate the image of a sincere, misunderstood peace advocate. So the second Reagan administration started with the boost of a landslide vote, but high on the list of public expectations was movement toward arms control. High on the list of public fears was the sending of U.S. troops into combat in Central America or elsewhere.

After the experience of the first four years, the Reagan approach has continued to be an aggressive pursuit of every opportunity to advance its unchanged strategic programs, mitigated by a proven ability to adjust its practical positions when unpleasant realities cannot be surmounted.

In these circumstances, what happens with Nicaragua takes on enormous importance, not only for the present but as a touchstone of the future. Unfortunately, we cannot dismiss the impact that the Reagan administration's massive pressure will have on the outcome. But we can say something with certainty: if Nicaragua remains standing after Reagan has made so absolute a commitment to its downfall, it will be proof indeed that the Cold War formula is no longer effective.

In focusing on Reagan, we invite two counter-sallies: First, there would not be a Cold War without the Soviets. Second, the Cold War has been as much, if not more, a Democratic as a Republican mission. Both of these observations carry truth, but both also cover up important truths.

How do Soviet perceptions fit into prospects for ending the Cold War?

The key requirement for a break with the Cold War is that each superpower adjust its ambitions and its policies to a changed world reality, and that neither retain the illusion that it can force the other into submission. By that standard, the Soviet leadership seems considerably more realistic and less reckless than the Reagan administration has been. There is no indication that the Soviets believe that they can establish military or technological superiority over the United States, that they bank on being able to pressure and subvert the United States into collapse, that they think they have the capacity to exclude U.S. interests from the third world. Yet the reverse of these ambitions is the barely hidden passion of Ronald Reagan.

Today, independent of divergent ideologies and social systems,

peace is inevitably menaced by any government that sees its
security embodied in anything like the level of death and destruction that defines a superpower. The Soviet government's military
emphasis, the priority it places on its superpower status, its deter-
mination not to lose control of countries within its sphere, its fear of
lowering barriers to alien influences—all of these feed on, and are
fed by, the Cold War.

Embedded in the Soviet view of Russian history and of the
postrevolutionary experience is the absolute resolve not to fall
behind in the arms race. That impulse is no less risky and burden-
some, even if less ambitious, than the goal of military supremacy is
for the United States. At the same time, the Soviet Union is
permeated with a searing memory and fear of war. The overkill
capacity of both sides contributes to the world's terror, but it is the
Reagan administration that has pushed the competitive military
build-up to new frontiers and has regarded arms control as the
enemy (cf. Strobe Talbott, *Deadly Gambits* [New York: Knopf,
1984]). Ronald Reagan's enthusiasm for accelerating the Great
Contest and projecting it into outer space is clearly not shared by
the Soviet Union.

The process of backing away from the Cold War does not need to
await fundamental alterations in the structure of Soviet or U.S.
society. In fact, adherence to such dogma on either side is the most
unrealistic and provocative course of all, one that in practice
accepts the inevitability of war. The end of the Cold War can
influence conditions that may ultimately result in fundamental
changes in the two societies, as well as in other countries. It is
unlikely, however, that there is world enough and time for things
to go the other way around.

The recognition that basic antagonisms between the two societies will persist does not mean that the context in which they are
expressed cannot change. That is exactly what is changing. It is
not a historical novelty for nations to accommodate, however
reluctantly, to sweeping changes in world power relationships
without undergoing internal upheaval and social transformation.
Of course, acceptance of such new realities generally has followed
wars or the rebellion of colonies. It remains to be seen whether
equivalent influence can be exerted by the now total threat to

survival, the diminishing capacity to control the third world, the failure and escalating burdens of the Great Contest.

In any case, a real advance toward peace is a very tall order. It can hardly come about without big political adjustments in the United States and in the Soviet Union.

How difficult will political change be in the United States? Without the build-up of political pressures and movements at least as strong and as varied as those in the final stages of the Vietnam war, retreat from the Cold War, from the arms race, and from military adventurism in Central America will be slow indeed.

Despite the genuine anxiety that Reagan's extreme militarism has produced among top Democrats, Mondale's ambiguity during the campaign debates was compounded of lingering Cold War loyalties and obeisance to anti-Communist orthodoxy. There is no doubt that there are very significant differences in judgment about today's world, about what can be risked and what should not. Reaganism unbridled is capable of frightening almost everyone to the left of Secretary of Defense Caspar Weinberger, but when the administration shows that it can side step, respectable liberal opposition loses some of its zest.

The hope for a political turnabout resides in the potential of movements that are still in the minority from the standpoint of organized political expression. In terms of public opinion, they reflect some majority and some minority positions. But the power of peace movements, of women's movements, of the idea of the Rainbow can be formidable.

I do not minimize Reagan's spectacular exploitation of the long-term impact of anti-Communism on U.S. politics. It is not reasonable to anticipate a new political majority without the prospect of relearning some bitter lessons that have faded in the Reagan era.

One can hope that the new failures from which we will have to learn are less than full repeats of past tragedies, military or economic. In any event, Reagan's act will be a hard one to follow. If he does not lead us to the last big bang, his presidency could be remembered as the last great hurrah of the Cold War era.

# DIANA JOHNSTONE

Author; European editor, *In These Times*

# For a New Political Culture

There are a few points of contrast between the first Cold War and the present one that I would like to emphasize.

The first is economic. At the end of World War II, the United States stood more or less alone, with a huge productive capacity in need of trading partners to avoid falling back into depression. Thus for the sake of the U.S. economy it was necessary to ship resources to Western Europe to speed European economic recovery. The Marshall Plan was the necessary solution. The United States distributed chips to the European players to keep them in the capitalist game. Although it was in the interests of U.S. business, the Marshall Plan was nevertheless generous enough to arouse, on the one hand, enthusiastic support in Europe and, on the other, opposition in the United States. To get the European recovery program through Congress, it was politically necessary to drama-tize the situation as yet another instance of the United States saving Europe from an evil threat to freedom—not Hitler anymore, but Communism ideologically equated with Naziism, thanks to the concept of totalitarianism.

To a very large extent, perhaps even entirely, the threats of war in Europe during Cold War I were a bluff to ease the passage of economic policies in both of the dominant blocs that had emerged from the war. These policies offered considerable advantages to a majority of the social forces in Western Europe. The war scare of the 1950s and the Soviet-inspired peace campaigns were, to some extent, part of an unsuccessful Soviet attempt to build political opposition to the U.S. economic programs that assured U.S. hegemony over Western Europe. In short, Cold War I offered

61

Western Europe great economic benefits at very little real risk
considering the overwhelming U.S. military and, especially, nuclear superiority at the time. Thus European leaders were, at the
start, enthusiastic partners on the U.S. side of Cold War I. For the
Italian Christian Democrats, it provided a way of keeping the left
out of office and themselves in, a way that has endured to this day.
In both Italy and France, it gave centrist political leaders a way of
depriving the Communists of the political share of influence they
had won through their leading role in the anti-Fascist resistance.
For Conrad Adenauer, it was a way to transform Germany from a
defeated enemy into an ally.

It is clear that Cold War II is not at all a repetition of Cold War I.
The major significant economic difference is that this time the
United States is not offering massive capital investment and a
share in economic prosperity to its European allies, but, on the
contrary, massive drain of investment capital out of Europe into
the United States, deepening unemployment, and the prospect of a
sharpening trade war. So, unlike Cold War I, Cold War II offers
Europe a more harrowing war scare without the economic re-
wards. The only benefits are political—the revival of anti-Communism which may be of use to certain political forces, especially far-
right political forces, inside various European countries. If most
European leaders seem to be going along, it is not because they
have anything to gain, but because they are afraid of a direct
confrontation with U.S. power and also because they have not
been able to figure out solutions of their own to the current
economic crisis. But U.S. policies, far from helping, are in fact
ruining the United States' European allies. This is a first significant difference between Cold War I and Cold War II.

A second difference is that this time around the United States is
hardly pretending to promote political freedom in the world. Instead, the U.S. representative at the United Nations draws spe-
cious distinctions between authoritarian and totalitarian regimes.
After World War II, the official ideology of the United States was
anti-colonialism. Now the United States is carrying out a massive
attack against the formerly colonialized countries known as the
third world, an attack that amounts to an effort to restore the
unhindered dominance of the imperialist power centers over the

third world. The exclusive aim of Reagan administration policy is not the old familiar imperialist goal—control of markets—but rather unhindered access to resources, especially oil and supposedly strategic minerals (which, incidentally, are used in the construction of a gigantic military machine to protect the access to strategic minerals, and so on and on in an absurd vicious circle); also access to, and control of, third world crop lands which used to nourish, perhaps poorly but to some extent, third world peoples before these lands were taken over by agribusiness for producing export crops. The United States is now fighting to make the world free for famine.

A third difference, which follows from those already mentioned, is that in Cold War I the United States used the United Nations as an instrument of policy, whereas now it is deliberately breaking down the United Nations system. At the height of Cold War I, the President was Eisenhower, a man who, after all, retired with a warning against the growing power of the military-industrial complex; whereas now we have a President who is really nothing but a front man for the military-industrial complex. All this means that the political isolation of the United States leadership is much greater—and potentially greater still—than in Cold War I.

The political problem for U.S. domestic resistance to Reagan administration policies is to find ways to link up with resistance abroad rather than allowing the right wing to go on using this foreign resistance to whip up a supporting chauvinism in the United States, as has been going on since the Iranian revolution. As in Cold War I, the heart of cold war is supposed to be the confrontation between the United States and the Soviet Union. As before, I think there is a great deal of bluff in this, although the bluff has changed and is increasingly dangerous. There is bluff now because in the last analysis the Reagan administration is not really arming to defend the United States from the Soviet threat, but as an economic development strategy and in order to be the top world power. The Soviet threat is the necessary political excuse and tends to become real insofar as the Soviet Union inevitably follows the U.S. lead in the arms race and may even occasionally get a step ahead in one field or another and that, in fact, represents an inherent threat to its neighbors.

This threat could best be reduced by a disarmament process, which the United States is more opposed to than ever. The technological optimists in power in Washington have decided instead to go all out for military superiority. Even arms control—much less disarmament—is being sacrificed to this attempt. The arms race, led by the United States, is not only between the United States and the Soviet Union. The whole world is drawn into it. Every country, however poor, must be encouraged to buy arms to help offset the cost of the arms-producing powers. Japan is being obliged to rearm; Western Europe is being encouraged to become a third nuclear superpower. The breakdown of the nuclear nonproliferation treaty is now practically a foregone conclusion. Since the Soviet-American conflict is largely a pretext for a development strategy led by weapons technology, it is not certain that pursuit of this course will necessarily culminate in the catastrophe of nuclear war between the United States and the Soviet Union. Even so, it is almost certain to produce other disasters.

The first certain disaster to be produced by this strategy is economic. The arms build-up is an economic strategy that cannot solve the problems of unemployment and inflation. At most, it can temporarily shift the worst effects to other countries, as in the case of Reagan's reelection year prosperity bubble, financed by investment capital drained from Europe by high interest rates combined with the mammoth U.S. budget deficit. But in the not so long run, the pouring of resources into arms manufacture can only aggravate basic economic problems.

The second disaster is political. What is being created is a sort of technological feudalism, a remilitarization of the world that can undo much of the political liberation of the past two or three centuries. As for the disaster of all-out nuclear war, it is made more likely by these factors of economic and political regression that are resulting from the arms race. The Reagan administration's declaratory policy toward the Soviet Union seems to increase the danger of war with that nation. It has recently become official policy to change the political order in Eastern Europe. Also, the Pentagon strategy of horizontal escalation now openly threatens to carry hostilities into relatively weak points of Soviet domination, notably Poland, in case of confrontation in some other region, such as the

Arab Persian Gulf. Many West Germans who would find themselves in the front lines in case of a horizontal escalation of a World
War III into Europe are afraid that this is not merely bluff.

On the other hand, many politically sophisticated observers
believe that these more or less veiled threats and pressures are
merely a sort of softening up process before U.S. diplomats sit
down with the Russians to negotiate a new Yalta, meaning a global
spheres of influence agreement. The French, in particular, have
tended to interpret Reagan administration policy as the preliminary to getting Moscow to accept the sort of linkage demanded by
Henry Kissinger. U.S. experts have to know that the Soviet Union
is neither as revolutionary nor as monolithic as official propagan-
dists make out. The far left in the West has long criticized Soviet
leaders for their conservatism, for selling out revolution. U.S.
strategists who do not even believe in genuine revolution are
naturally even more skeptical of Soviet devotion to Communism
and more cynically certain that the Kremlin reasons solely in terms
of national interest. The goal of U.S. policy is thus to encourage the
nationalist strain over the Communist-internationalist strain in the
Soviet leadership. This seems to offer some prospect of success
because it is costly to the Soviet Union to aid countries like
Vietnam and, indeed, the sacrifices involved tend to be resented by
much of the Russian population. Kissinger has said that the Soviet
Union must decide whether it is a country or a cause. If it would
just be a conservative nationalist military dictatorship like any
other country, then the promise is implicit that it might be allowed
its place as a European power.

The point I wish to make is that, as with the rest of the world,
whether deliberately or inadvertently, current U.S. policy favors
not the liberalization but the militarization of the Soviet Union.
This time, as I said, the United States has no Marshall Plan, no
economic recovery benefits, to offer its European allies. Instead, it
is offering a piece of the action in imperialist restoration with
invitations to go along on expeditions to Lebanon and other trouble
spots.

Now in Europe a whole range of right wing forces are crawling
out of the woodwork to take advantage of the historic opportunity
offered by the Reagan administration. Reagan exemplifies the

combination of two kinds of power used together—weaponry and imagery—both in their contemporary technological versions. There are all sorts of ultra-right authoritarians, royalists who dream of restoring the Holy Roman Empire, or genetic engineering elitists—all are enthusiastic about Ronald Reagan. He shows them a new way to dominate the masses through manipulation of television images.

In Europe, then, political forces are not polarized between pro-United States and pro-Soviet positions, as in Cold War I. Except in Italy, where the Communist Party practically *is* the left, the new peace movements are not led by Communists and nowhere are they pro-Soviet, as they were in the 1950s. This time, the political forces in Europe which correspond roughly to U.S.-style political liberalism are very largely opposed to U.S. policy. This is an important difference, I think. Through the 1970s, there was a general breakdown of the old left that was associated with the pro-Soviet, Communist parties in the West, and there were various movements and forces which represented a sort of splitting up of the left movements. The peace issue is the key to the recomposition of the left. The ecology movement, the women's movement, the labor movement—around the issue of conversion of industry—as well as farmers' movements and third world support movements, can all come together around the life-and-death issue of peace. There can also perhaps be an international recomposition, but for this to be achieved there needs to be a strong U.S. component in these movements.

I have not emphasized as much as I would like to how much I really think that the third world is the key to the Cold War. It can also be a key to the question of what lies beyond the Cold War. I think that viewed from a long-term perspective, the East-West confrontation will probably vanish, as other such confrontations have vanished, because new problems arise—not because there is ever a solution, but because people start to worry about something else. The religious wars between Protestantism and Catholicism were not settled by the victory of one side or the other. People just forgot about that and started fighting about something different. I think that in the long sweep of history, the differences between bourgeois democracy and the working-class Marxist movement are going to appear as two aspects of the same moment in history, products of a particular stage of industrial development. This conflict is just going to wear out—if it is allowed to wear out, and if people turn their attention to the other problems that are facing us.

The present global crisis is, in fact, a whole conglomerate of these new problems—some of which have not even been named yet—ecology being one that has come most sharply into focus. The German peace movement is, to my mind, the first hopeful sign because it is bringing together a lot of things. It is not just an ecology movement; it is a movement that is using various traditions of political struggle and political analysis to address the real problems of today—not the ideological problems that are left over, but the real problems: peace and environment, the question of the third world. Also, it is not only addressing them in the abstract, but there is a great deal of intellectual work and concrete analysis of these problems being done, looking for real solutions, and these solutions are very radical. They do demand a new way of life.

The first question is: Why all of this arms race in order to protect access to resources? Well, why? Because we are wasting all these resources. If we would just learn to live with what we have at home, we would not have to be going all over the world to protect "our" resources which are located, it so happens, everywhere else. That is the necessary cultural change, but there are also transitional programs that are coming out of the German left. There is Willy Brandt's proposal for shifting 5 percent from arms expenditure to third world development. It is a modest figure, but the figure does not matter so much. It is the idea of this shift, of changing direction. This is a very small and reasonable proposal, but it *is* supported by important political forces in Northern Europe, in the Social Democratic parties. This is something that can be connected to on an international scale.

There has to be an end to the Alice's tea-party approach that the United States uses: you just keep dirtying the dishes, moving on along the table, thinking you will never get around to where you started. There is a tremendous need to build a new political culture, a new political sensitivity to real problems. I think this has begun in Germany. I think there are enough similarities between the situation in Germany and that in the United States, even though they are very different, for there to be some reason to hope something similar can develop here. We can get up at a conference and somebody can have a wonderful idea and a wonderful program, but that is not really enough. You have to have a political culture, that is to say, masses of people who understand these questions thoroughly, who offer solutions and who will fight for them. It is not a matter of somebody having an idea; it is a matter of developing complex responses to very complex problems within the social forces that then are prepared to fight for them. Otherwise you just have what you have now, which is the right wing in charge of policy virtually by default because democratic processes of decision making are simply nonexistent in these fields. These have to be created from the bottom by a lot of this sort of thing, by a lot of institutes like the Institute for Policy Studies, by a lot of newspapers like *In These Times*. It is just pathetic what little resources we, who are trying to think of these things independently, have compared to those working for the arms industry. There has to be a large public that will support this kind of activity, this collective thinking, this collective change of political culture.

# MICHAEL T. KLARE

Five College Associate Professor of Peace
and World Security Studies, Hampshire College;
defense correspondent, *Nation*

# The Third World Arena

[. . .] Since the 1950s, the most virulent and violent manifestations of the Cold War have been in the third world.

Why is this so? There are a number of reasons why I think this is the case. The most important is that the main perceived arena of conflict—Europe—was largely stabilized by 1950. For better or worse, the creation of NATO and the Warsaw Pact, and the development of nuclear arsenals on both sides, have stabilized that arena of confrontation, and both sides are well aware of the suicidal risks of conducting a conflict in that area. So there has been a tendency to deflect the intensity and friction of conflict between the two blocs to those areas where the risks for either side are much less—and that means in the third world. And so we have seen two major wars fought by the United States since World War II that in many ways were a manifestation of the Cold War between the superpowers, but were fought in the third world. These wars—Korea and Vietnam—were perceived as surrogate conflicts for the direct East-West clash that both sides were afraid of. Now we are on the verge of another example of this in Central America where, at least from the U.S. point of view, a third world conflict is being defined as an expression of the Cold War.

Another reason why the third world has been an arena of Cold War conflict is precisely because it has not been divided neatly by the World War II divisions that you have in Europe and Korea. The lines are more fluid, and therefore the struggles that occur in the third world take on greater symbolic importance. The gains or losses, as they are perceived, become indicators of U.S. or Soviet gains in the great Cold War sweepstakes. That is happening in

69

Central America now, where a struggle that at other times in U.S. history would be perceived as peripheral is being perceived as a new Cold War challenge. This has occurred periodically throughout the history of the Cold War. A perceived gain by the Soviet Union in Africa or the Middle East or the Caribbean takes on a symbolic importance because of the very fluidity of the lines. Actually, there are constant changes in the alignments between East and West in the third world, but when these alignments occur at moments of crisis or of heightened superpower conflict, they often become the trigger for East-West, U.S.-Soviet conflict.

I also think that both the Soviet Union and the United States have reasons of their own for looking at the third world as a substitute arena for military conflict. On the part of the Soviet Union I think the motives are, precisely, to escape from containment and encirclement. After World War II and the anti-Soviet security pacts of the John Foster Dulles days, the Soviet Union felt surrounded, and its opportunities for gaining influence in Europe and in Asia pretty much circumscribed, by these pacts and alliances. And so the only way that the Soviet Union was able to achieve new influence in the world and widen its political horizons was to "leapfrog" over the lines that had been established by the United States on its periphery—in other words, to go into the third world and seek new opportunities for influence and political gains.

From the U.S. side there is a somewhat different motivation, and that is, if you will, "imperial peace-keeping." With the decline of the European imperial systems in the third world after World War II, U.S. leaders perceived themselves as assuming the responsibility for maintaining "law and order" in the third world, and ensuring that third world countries remained within the world capitalist system. We call that world policing or world peacekeeping. But that task was not something that could easily be sold to the U.S. public on its own terms. That was imperialism, that was colonialism, and those are things that the U.S. people historically have refused to support. So in order to provide legitimacy for this continuing role of peacekeeping in the third world, the United States has consistently defined these policing missions as manifestations of the U.S.-Soviet competition. And that is exactly what is happening in Central America today. I think it is clear to everyone that the origins of the struggle in Central America are rooted in the historical situation of the countries involved; but for the United States to go in as Ronald Reagan would like and act as the regional police power would appear to be an imperialistic intervention, and the public will not support that. So the only way you could get political legitimacy for such an act would be to describe it as a response to Soviet aggression.[. . .]

What are the costs for us? Typically, it is customary to think of this deflection of the Cold War to the third world as, in some sense, a gain for the United States and the Soviet Union. And I think it would be naive to deny that, on balance, if the third world had not been there to fight out the Cold War for us, it probably would have been fought out at some point or another in Europe, and that could have triggered a catastrophic nuclear conflict. So this country and the Soviet Union have in some sense benefited from the shunting of our Cold War conflicts to the third world. But I want to argue that the long-term price we are going to pay for this will be equally great. I am convinced that the arming of the third world is another form of global self-destruction that the Cold War is contributing to. The long-term effect of global militarization, of supplying third world countries with sophisticated conventional weapons, represents a danger to world stability almost as great as the nuclear arms race itself. We are just beginning to see what that could possibly mean in the Middle East. Conflict is still at a relatively moderate level, but is escalating rapidly. And down the road, our wars in the third world are going to be fought at levels of violence comparable to what we would expect in a NATO–Warsaw Pact conventional war. This is the kind of situation that more than anything else is likely to provide the tinder and the spark that will ignite a World War III in which we will all perish. And even if that does not happen, conflicts in the third world are going to threaten world stability on their own terms, in a general level of global violence in which none of the countries of the world will make any progress.

# PATRICIA FLYNN

Author; staff member,
Center for the Study of the Americas

# Expansionism and National Security

What I would like to do is to try to turn the Cold War argument of the Reagan administration on its head, so to speak, and to argue that the real threat in the Caribbean and Central America is not Soviet-Cuban expansionism, but rather U.S. expansionism. In fact, what we are witnessing is a case where the accuser is guilty of the crime. It is the United States and *not* the Soviet Union that is intervening massively in the region. It is the United States that is trying to force acceptance of its ideology and its economic and political system on the countries and revolutionary movements of the region. It is the United States which has created an army of insurgents—who I think would most appropriately be called terrorists—that is trying to topple a legitimate government in Nicaragua. And it is the United States and not the Soviet Union that is building military bases and airfields, that has dispatched warships to the region, and that has finally sent in an invading force.[. . .]

The United States defines its national interest as having complete political, economic, and military domination over Central America. While that argument is often phrased in terms of a Cold War framework and a Cold War logic, I believe that the East-West competition is something of a straw man in this whole argument. In fact, I think that what is more important to the United States is that Central America is at the heart of what could be called its "informal empire," which is the essence of what Reagan means by our "backyard." For nearly a century, the United States has dominated the region, politically and economically, and it views the loss of exclusive political control as a threat to its world power. Economically, the region is extremely important to the United

States: if you take the region as a whole, there are $17 billion in U.S. holdings there (and that does not include Puerto Rico). And of course the U.S. military wants exclusive access to the area, an area that it views as strategic to its ability to wage war around the world.

Essentially, by this definition of the national interest the United States is telling Central America and the Caribbean that it is the U.S. national interest, and not the interests of the people and nations of the region, that is to take precedence. If Central America is to be removed from the arena of the Cold War, it will mean challenging this basic definition of U.S. national security, which is accepted not just by the Reagan administration but by the Democratic Party as well. Up to now, the consequence for any nation in the region that has chosen to be in conflict with that definition of U.S. national security has been swift retaliation, as we have seen most recently in Grenada.[. . .]

# TOM WICKER

Editorial columnist, *New York Times*

## Will We Tolerate Marxist Governments in This Hemisphere?

[. . .] I think there is no question that in the Cold War politics of the world, Central America is vitally involved. In fact, I am quite pessimistic about any efforts to extricate Central America from that Cold War context, for the reason that I think the situation there takes on an importance beyond the mere fact that Nicaragua may be Marxist. It takes on an importance beyond that to the Reagan administration, which regards Central America in far more symbolic geopolitical terms than the mere question of whether there is a Marxist government there or not. Alexander Haig, one of the architects of the Reagan administration's policy in the region, spoke quite frankly. He said our interests there are first global, second regional, and third local. Which puts those countries in a rather crude perspective, but I think that is the way the Reagan administration looks at them. Former Secretary of State Henry Kissinger is on record as saying (before his current service as head of the President's Commission) that if we cannot control events in Central America, who will believe that we can control them in the Persian Gulf? And President Reagan said in his Spring 1983 speech to Congress on the Central American question that if we cannot defend ourselves there, we cannot expect to prevail elsewhere.

I think that it is this geopolitical view that dominates thinking about Central America in Washington. The idea is that everything we do is a message in some form to the Soviet Union and to all the countries that are of importance to us; that if we show weakness in Central America, we will somehow be regarded as a weak state; that if we can crush Grenada—that powerful bastion of Communism in the Caribbean—somehow we will be accepted as a strong state; that these messages are really what the game is all about. I think that was the major reason for the invasion of Grenada—this belief that somehow the United States will be perceived as weak, despite Minuteman missiles, despite all of our weapons, despite all of our warships. That somehow we will be perceived as weak if we back away from untenable positions, taken anywhere; or if we fail to prevail in every encounter or challenge that we may have with a country that can be regarded as an adversary. I say that that is the *true* "Vietnam syndrome," which extended that war for at least five or six years beyond reasonable expectations of victory. The true Vietnam syndrome is this feeling that somehow we cannot afford to lose anywhere. We cannot afford to back away, we cannot afford to be seen as not having prevailed, because then we will be seen as weak and people will move against us from all directions. It surpasses my imagination how after forty years of Cold War the United States could be perceived by any nation as weak or lacking in will to pursue its interests; but it is upon that fear that much of U.S. policy has been based in recent years.

I think another reason why it is going to be difficult to extricate Central America from the Cold War context is because of an unsettled question that runs very deep into the U.S. grain: the question of Marxism/Communism in the Western Hemisphere. Are we going to tolerate Communist or Marxist countries in the Western Hemisphere? Since the 1962 Cuban missile crisis, and the tacit agreements that followed it, the United States has tolerated Cuba as a Marxist state in the Caribbean. I think probably it will continue to do so, not just because of that agreement but because it obviously is a difficult, bloody, and costly problem to try to overthrow that government. But in 1954 we did overthrow what was regarded as a Marxist government in Guatemala. We helped to overthrow an elected Marxist government in Chile in 1971. We are assisting the fight in El Salvador, sponsoring the fight in Nicaragua, and we invaded Grenada—all adding up to the resounding policy decision that *no,* we will not tolerate more Communist states in the Western hemisphere.

But the mere posing of the question, "Will we tolerate Communist states in the Western hemisphere?" poses other questions

difficult to answer. Does the mere existence of a Marxist government in Nicaragua post a threat to the United States? To the
neighbors of Nicaragua, does it mean that there is inevitably going
to be some kind of domino theory at work, so that all states up to the
Rio Grande will steadily become Communist if we allow even one
to do so? Does it mean there will be an effort on the part of
Nicaragua, aided by Cuba, to set such a row of falling dominoes in
motion? And another question: Would we really tolerate Nicaragua and have satisfactory relations with it, if it minded its own
business, left its neighbors alone, and was simply a Marxist state
trying to survive and serve its people in Central America? I do not
think that these are questions that can easily be answered. The
undersecretary of defense, Fred Ikle, said in a public statement
approved by the White House that the aim of the United States in
Nicaragua is to *prevent* the consolidation of the Sandinista regime.
I do not know how you can read that in any other way than its
overthrow. And he said that we are seeking a military victory in
Central America.

Other questions are raised by that basic question of whether or
not we will tolerate Marxist/Communist governments in the Western hemisphere. If we will not, if the answer is the answer we gave
to Guatemala, and are now trying to give to Nicaragua, then to
what extent should we or will we tolerate abuses of human rights
on the part of allied governments in order to keep Communism out
of the hemisphere? That question applies at this very moment, and
in the sharpest fashion, to Guatemala. It applies to Chile; it applies
to El Salvador; and it did apply, until 1979, to Nicaragua under
Somoza.

If we will not permit Marxist regimes in the Western hemisphere, does that proscription not also imply the use at some point
of our own armed forces to prevent such regimes from taking or
holding power? If a Marxist regime truly did threaten the vital
interests of the United States just by existing, let alone by trying to
export its ideology, would those vital interests not demand protection by whatever degree of armed force necessary?

Finally, I raise a somewhat less direct question, but one not less
interesting and not less important. Is Communism in this sense, in
the sense of the geopolitical aspects of U.S. policy in Central

America, something of a straw man? The real U.S. aim, over more than a century in Central America, has been, I think, primarily to have governments there that are responsive to U.S. influence—to have influence over those governments in order to be able to say that Central America is indeed our backyard, that it is an area of the world where our influence is dominant, and will be dominant, and must be dominant. Is the fear of Communism and the geopolitical emphasis really a straw man, a beard, so to speak, for that sort of attitude? I think it may be, and if that is the case, obviously Marxist governments simply cannot be tolerated.

So I think all of these questions arise from that one basic question: Will the United States be willing in the years ahead to tolerate Marxist governments in the Western hemisphere if they arise, or are we going to take the attitude that that is the one thing that we will not tolerate? I want to emphasize that I am not talking about Soviet bases in Central America, which obviously would be a different matter. I am raising the question that it is perhaps most necessary to answer, whether we will in the long run say that this is a hemisphere that is off-limits to Communism no matter what the United States has to do to stop it.

# T H E

# F U T U R E
# O F   T H E
# C O L D
# W A R

## P A R T   2

Do you think peaceful termination
of the Cold War is a real possibility
in the foreseeable future?

If so, under what circumstances?

# STANLEY HOFFMANN

Douglas Dillon Professor of the Civilization of France;
Chairman, Center for European Studies, Harvard University

[. . .] I can give you a very brief summary of my view. I think peaceful termination of the Cold War is possible under one of two sets of circumstances. It could end, in the first place, if the superpowers decided to practice what I have called elsewhere a détente without illusions. This would have to entail both very extensive arms control and reduction agreements, and a policy of large-scale economic and political cooperation, so as to avoid and manage the crises which the inevitable rivalry between the great powers and the efforts of their clients to implicate them will undoubtedly provoke. In the second place, the Cold War could come to a peaceful end from the bottom, so to speak, rather than from the top, if each of the two rivals gets increasingly concerned with its own domestic problems and finds itself giving priority abroad to issues in which the chief rival plays only an insignificant role. The second hypothesis strikes me as more likely than the first. You can guess from my reply that I make a distinction between the contest of the superpowers, which I consider to be of very long duration, and the Cold War itself, which I would define as an exacerbated, although predominantly nonviolent, form of this contest—one in which coexistence is preserved but cooperation is largely absent.

# STROBE TALBOTT

Author; journalist; editor, *Time*

*[This is the transcript of a phone conversation between Strobe Talbott and Leon Wofsy.]*

*Strobe Talbott:* Do I think peaceful termination of the Cold War is a real possibility in the foreseeable future? I have a problem with that kind of question. It is an old dodge, but it all depends on what you mean by Cold War; it all depends on what you mean by terminate; I suppose it all depends on what you mean by the foreseeable future. The definition of the Cold War is the main problem. If by Cold War one means a state of tensions and acute disagreement and conflict of national interests between the superpowers, then I do *not* think it is possible to terminate that. I think that is a state of affairs that is, at least in its most basic formulation, part and parcel of the relationship. It stems from the irreconcilable differences between the nature of the two societies and, to an arguably somewhat lesser extent, their interests and objectives in the world. But the really fundamental problem is the way in which the societies are organized. It makes it impossible to have what you might call warm peace between them.

*LW:* Can one distinguish the irreconcilable differences from the Cold War form of that rivalry? That is, is it conceivable that while the basic conflicts would continue, the intensity of the military confrontation could in some way be lessened significantly?

*Strobe Talbott:* That certainly is possible and desirable and my guess is that something like that will occur. The military competition has, of course, a number of dimensions. The most commented on is the rivalry in the acquisition and deployment of strategic nuclear weapons, or nuclear weapons generally, and that is an area where there can be some important regulation and amelioration as a result of arms control. And while arms control has not fared very well in the last few years, it is not, by any means, at a dead end. There is some sign that it could get back on track, so there, I think, you could have an improvement.

*LW:* I guess the essential problem is whether the kind of political leaderships are possible in either country that would bring such improvement about in the next period without a fundamental upheaval in either society. And what that gets to, I suppose, is your view of whether either leadership now seriously wants a shift from the intensity of the military rivalry.

*Strobe Talbott:* Well, the U.S. leadership is torn by all kinds of internecine conflicts and disagreements, and by a fundamental ambivalence on the part of the President. But my own feeling is that, for political and other reasons, it is moving in the direction where it might be amenable to those kinds of arrangements. The Soviet leadership, I think, is definitely amenable to them, not because it is more virtuous than the Reagan administration, but because it has more compelling and obvious pressures on it to keep the arms race under some sort of control so that it can expend resources in other sectors of their economy.

*LW:* Then you feel there has been a significant shift in the attitude of the Reagan administration toward arms control since the time you wrote your book, that it is more favorable now than it was during its first term?

*Strobe Talbott:* Yes. A couple of things have changed. It is certainly more favorable than during the first term. In the paperback edition of *Deadly Gambits,* I actually wrote an epilogue that made the point that I am making now, namely that for reasons of alliance solidarity, for domestic political reasons, and for reasons having to do with the appreciation on the part of some people in the administration that they have a great opportunity as a result of Star Wars, there is a body of opinion within the administration that would like to take advantage of the leverage that Star Wars gives them and get a deal sometime during the second term. That is not a unanimous view, and it is not clear yet whether it is going to be the view of the President, but it is still a view that is in the ascendant.

*LW:* Do you think that the impact of the Reagan administration on the relationship between the United States and the Soviet Union has a long-term quality? In other words, once Reagan leaves the scene, do you think it would be possible or likely that there would be any substantial shift in the posture of the United States toward relations with the Soviet Union?

*Strobe Talbott:* If it were President Kemp, I would have one set of expectations; if it were President Bush or President Cuomo, I would have very different expectations. But I think whoever is President, the trends that I am talking about are still going to be there.

*LW:* Do you have any opinion about the present set of disagreements between Macfarlane and the Soviet military on the 1972 ABM treaty? How serious do you think the Soviet test ban pronouncement and proposals on nuclear arms reduction are?

*Strobe Talbott:* Well, those are obviously different issues. On the degree to which the Strategic Defense Initiative (SDI) is permissable under the 1972 treaty, I think that Macfarlane's public statements are simply not supportable, either against the historical record or against a common sense reading of the language of the 1972 treaty. On the latter issue, I think that the Soviet initiative for a moratorium was sincere in that they really wanted it to happen, but that it was rigged, as these things very often are, and it was billed very much as a public ploy, which is one reason the administration renounced it as quickly as it did. It was clearly intended, among other things, to inhibit SDI, one aspect of which is the development of a nuclear-driven X-ray laser that has to be tested underground, and which would be prohibited under the terms of the Soviet proposal.

*LW:* At this point, could you estimate what you think the objectives in the Cold War are, for both the U.S. and the Soviet leaderships; in other words, what their terms would be, what they hope to accomplish.

*Strobe Talbott:* Well, each wants to circumscribe, and if possible reduce, the international influence of the other, and to weaken, if not bring about, the collapse of the internal structure of the other— I mean in its darkest terms.

*LW:* It seems that the Soviet Union must be much less motivated by such hopes at this point than is the Reagan administration.

*Strobe Talbott:* I think that is correct.

# HANS A. BETHE

Professor and Nobel Laureate,
Newman Laboratory of Nuclear Studies,
Cornell University

In answer to your letter, I do think that a peaceful termination of the Cold War is a real possibility. It is uncertain of course when this will happen, and even if it does happen it is quite possible that the Cold War may be restarted. For instance, after Nixon's visit to the Soviet Union, and the Vladivostok agreement, I believe the Cold War was suspended for nearly ten years, until President Reagan restarted it.

The circumstance which I consider necessary is that leaders of both countries be sincerely devoted to terminating the Cold War. It is difficult to read the intentions of any Soviet statesman, but at least I have the impression that Gorbachev has a desire to stop the Cold War. He is young and vigorous enough to last for many years in his position. During this period, I hope and believe, a President will be elected in the United States who has the same desire and enough authority to persuade the U.S. people that détente is the only sensible way for the two countries to live together. The President would have to be a man like Franklin Roosevelt, both in his convictions and his persuasive power.

The social structure and long-range political aims of the Soviet Union and the United States are likely to remain very different, and contradictory, for many decades to come. But it seems to me that the desire for peace is very great in the United States as well as in the Soviet Union.

# NOAM CHOMSKY

Author; Professor of Linguistics and Philosophy,
Massachusetts Institute of Technology

I see no possibility that Cold War tensions can be significantly reduced in the foreseeable future. The reasons are basically two. First, each superpower is, in fact, an impediment to the ambitions of the other. Second, despite the fundamental conflict, each has come to rely on the other's existence, and its brutality, for its own purposes.

The first point is relatively transparent. The primary goal of the military-bureaucratic elite that rules the Soviet Union is to run its dungeon, including the East European satellites, without interference while seeking targets of opportunity elsewhere. It should be further noted that no Russian government will abandon control over Eastern Europe so long as a rearmed Germany remains part of a hostile Western alliance, for obvious historical and security reasons. Given this posture, the Soviet Union has generally favored détente: meaning a system of joint global management by the two superpowers, in which each concedes to the other an area of domination in which it may act without serious interference. The United States has generally rejected this arrangement, and thus stands as a barrier to Soviet policy.

U.S. goals have been more expansive. The United States emerged from World War II in a position of global dominance with few if any historical parallels, and U.S. planners were determined to ensure that the United States would remain the "hegemonic power in a system of world order," in the words of a 1975 Trilateral Commission study, deploring the decline of this system. Planners sought to construct what they called a "Grand Area," a region subordinated to the needs of the U.S. economy, including at a minimum the

Western hemisphere, the Far East, and the former British empire, as well as the Middle East and Western Europe. Early goals were to assure access to Eurasian resources quite generally. As George Kennan explained the matter in Policy Planning Study 23 (February 1948), the United States had 50 percent of the world's wealth but only 6 percent of its population, a fact that led to "envy and resentment": "Our real task in the coming period is to devise a pattern of relationships which will permit us to maintain this disparity. . . ." To do so, harsh measures will be necessary, and we must put aside such "vague" and "unreal" objectives as "human rights, the raising of living standards, and democratization": "The less we are then hampered by idealistic slogans, the better." The prescription was specifically for the Far East, but the United States is a global power, and in both planning and actual practice the doctrine extended worldwide, despite the regular resort to "idealistic slogans" for public consumption.

The primary U.S. objective was to ensure that within the Grand Area there would be no serious challenge to its dominance, no form of independent development. This is why the United States turned at once to a systematic program of destruction of the anti-fascist resistance in much of the world, often in favor of former fascist collaborators. One facet of this program was the use of Nazi war criminals of the Klaus Barbie variety, dispatched to Latin America when the trail got too hot, where they could continue their work in a manner that establishes a direct connection, via the United States, from the Nazis to the killing fields in Central America today. With regard to the Soviet Union, though the United States did toy with a "rollback" strategy in the early years (cf. NSC 68, 1950), and one hears echoes of this among more fanatic jingoist elements today, clearer minds understood that it was beyond the bounds of feasibility. The Soviet Union poses barriers to U.S. goals in two respects: by its existence, dominating a bloc that is not open to U.S. economic exploitation and political control, and by offering a measure of support to forces within U.S. domains that seek to pursue a path unacceptable to the United States.

Each superpower would undoubtedly prefer to see the other disappear, but each has come to understand that this is impossible short of mutual annihilation. The conflict has therefore settled into a system of hostility combined with mutual accommodation. This brings us to the second and more subtle point: the exploitation of the brutality of the enemy for the implementation of policy goals.

While on both sides the rhetoric of the Cold War focuses on the superpower enemy, the actual events of the Cold War yield a different picture. The substance of the Cold War system consists primarily of intervention and subversion by the two superpowers within their own domains: East Berlin, Hungary, Czechoslovakia, Poland, Afghanistan (the sole large-scale example of the use of Soviet forces beyond the borders conquered by the Red Army during World War II), Greece, Iran, Guatemala, Cuba, Indochina, the Dominican Republic, Chile, El Salvador, Nicaragua, and all too many others.

Any power, whether democratic or totalitarian, must find a way to mobilize public support, at home and among allies, for costly and brutal actions. Throughout history, the primary means for accomplishing this end has been the appeal to the threat of some Great Satan. Soviet interventions have been presented at home as defensive: the Soviet Union must defend itself from the threat posed by aggressive forces dominated by the global enemy. There is no such event as the "invasion of Afghanistan" in Soviet theology; rather, it is a "defense of Afghanistan" against terrorists supported by the CIA and other warmongers. Our doctrinal system is similar. Thus the U.S. attack against South Vietnam—beginning with bombing and defoliation in 1962 as part of an effort to drive millions of people into concentration camps after seven years of state terror, followed by direct invasion and expansion of the aggression to all of Indochina—literally does not exist in U.S. history; rather, there is a "defense of South Vietnam" against terrorists unleashed by the Soviet Union (in other variants, by China) and its client North Vietnam—a "defense" which, the doves contend, was unwise or excessively brutal. Throughout the history of the real Cold War, the same has been true.

The utility of the Great Satan extends further. The Soviet system is held under control by violence, so that its leaders naturally require a militarized society. The costs are severe, and the populace must agree to bear them. To some extent terror suffices, but a better method is acquiescence out of a perceived need to defend the society against the great enemy. As for the United States, it has been clearly recognized by government and business leaders that the state must intervene in the economy to stimulate production, and for a variety of reasons the Pentagon system was developed as the optimal means to achieve this result. This system funnels public subsidies to advanced sectors of industry, research, and development while assigning profits to the private sector during this phase and when commercial applications become possible. It is an elegant system of public subsidy, private profit. A state-guaranteed market for rapidly obsolescing high technology waste production (armaments) is optimally designed to benefit existing private power and privilege while offering minimal interference with the businessman's prerogatives. The long-term costs may be severe, but planning is not undertaken in this framework in a competitive society, and once the system is established, powerful vested interests ensure its maintenance. Again, the population must be willing to bear the costs. It is a rare political leader who will approach the public with the news that it is necessary for the poor to subsidize the wealthy (who control investment) for the ultimate health of the economy. It is much simpler to appeal to what the President has called the "monolithic and ruthless conspiracy" that aims to thwart our benevolence throughout the world—President Kennedy, in this case, as he initiated the vast military build-up that set off the current phase of the arms race under the pretext of a fraudulent "missile gap." His Keynesian successor Ronald Reagan behaves in much the same way, and indeed the same has been true throughout.

It is for this reason that the United States rejects any arms control agreement that would limit development of more advanced weapons systems, and concocts such fantasies as "Star Wars," a system designed to maintain the arms race and provide subsidies for the most advanced sectors of the high technology industry, which will be pursued regardless of the evident risks to national security that it entails. For the same reason, a nuclear freeze is not a policy option, despite support for it by some three-quarters of the population and its clear feasibility, given Soviet advocacy of this position and endorsement by a large majority of the United Nations. For the same reason, the United States cannot accept a ban on nuclear weapons or missile tests, though this would reduce the threat of the first strike that the Star Wars program theoretically aims to deter, at far less cost and risk and with no serious problem of verifiability. Neither public opinion nor feasibility nor security is a major concern; there are more important considerations. The United States will agree to a limitation on weapons; our comparative advantage is not in production but in advanced technology. But the system of state industrial management through the Pentagon can hardly face a challenge.

In short, the Cold War has evolved into a system of tacit cooperation, in which the leadership of each superpower exploits the violence and brutality of the enemy—real enough, in both cases—to achieve quite different purposes: intervention and militarization of the domestic society, in our case as a technique for compelling the public to invest in advanced sectors of the economy without sharing in the profits or interfering with management.

There is no space here to explore further complexities—which exist—or to document this history, but the essentials should be plain enough to those who choose to penetrate the rhetoric that clouds it.

The system is both costly and unstable. The major costs are borne by the victims of superpower intervention, but the domestic societies also bear a serious burden: material, cultural, and moral. Sooner or later the system is bound to collapse. The two greatest threats are technical advances in weaponry, which lead to increased reliance on automated rapid response systems, which raise the probability of war by error, inadvertence, or misjudgment in times of crisis; and the even more serious threat that tensions and conflicts in the third world may engage the superpowers and rapidly escalate, as has repeatedly come close in the past and will again—the Middle East being the primary "tinder box."

The Cold War system, then, is one of potential mutual suicide, and vast suffering, massacre, torture, starvation, semi-slave labor, and so on, throughout the dependent areas. There are indigenous causes too, but the contribution of the superpowers is not slight. Nevertheless, the Cold War system has a short-term rationality from the point of view of dominant groups in the two societies, and without significant institutional changes no serious alternative is in sight.

The bipolar world of the early postwar period has slowly eroded, as new centers of power developed in a more complex global system. The capacity of each superpower to coerce has steadily declined, while their absolute power to destroy continually increases. Serious conflicts are arising within the U.S.-dominated system, and are sure to increase, and there is a bare possibility that Europe and Japan may come to pursue a more independent course, with consequences that cannot be pursued here. But for the foreseeable future the Cold War system of global conflict and global management appears fairly stable, with the prospect of a terminal war, one of the ever present elements of this system, an increasing likelihood.

# PAUL M. SWEEZY

Co-editor, *Monthly Review*

How one answers the question of whether the peaceful termination of the Cold War is a real possibility in the foreseeable future, and if so under what circumstances, depends on one's analysis of the nature and causes of the Cold War.

There are, of course, many factors involved, and it would be a mistake to speak of *the* cause of the Cold War. In my opinion, however, there is no doubt that underlying all other considerations is a fundamental hostility of capitalism to the very existence of an alternative social system which is both viable on its own terms and able to resist penetration and absorption into the capitalist world order.

Whether the alternative system is socialist or not is not the issue. In my opinion, the Soviet Union is not socialist, at least not in the traditional Marxist sense, but neither is it capitalist. But it is viable, and it does resist penetration and absorption into the world capitalist system. Moreover, it acts as a pole of attraction for third world countries which are part of the periphery of world capitalism and are exploited and dominated by the metropolises at the center. For all these reasons, the Soviet Union is perceived as an enemy by the capitalist powers, and most especially by the United States, which is the largest and most powerful among these. What is of decisive importance is that this situation exists quite independently of the foreign and military policies pursued by the Soviet Union. As far as the United States is concerned, the Soviet Union is the enemy because it *exists*, not because of what it does. In its near seventy-year history, the Soviet Union has always been on the defensive and often under military attack. It has tried many tactics to blunt the thrust of capitalist hostility, consistently expressing its adherence to the doctrine of peaceful coexistence of countries with different social systems and in recent years proclaiming its readiness for a policy of détente and disarmament (or arms control) much more substantial than the capitalist powers have been willing to consider seriously. All in vain. The only exception was World War II when the capitalist powers (except Japan and Italy) became allied with the Soviet Union in what was for both a life-and-death struggle against Hitler's Germany. But no sooner were Germany and its allies defeated than the victors began to put pressure on the Soviet Union to retreat and give up any role in the organization of the postwar world. That was the real beginning of the Cold War, which has been going on ever since and has risen to new levels of intensity under the Reagan administration.

If this analysis is correct, it follows that the Cold War could be peacefully terminated tomorrow if the U.S. government so willed it. That this will not happen as long as Reagan is in the White House is obvious. The answer to the question posed at the outset is therefore that the Cold War can be peacefully terminated as soon as the United States installs a government that is willing to accept the existence of the Soviet Union on a live-and-let-live basis. Whether *this* is a possibility in the foreseeable future is an entirely different question—one to which I, for one, do not pretend to have the answer. It depends, I suppose, on the U.S. people coming to understand the real issues and their ability to organize and wage what at best could only be a long and bitter struggle to change the kind of government that has represented them ever since World War I.

# FLORA LEWIS

Foreign affairs columnist,
*New York Times*

[. . .] I will try to give you a quick sense of my views.

First, I think asking about "peaceful termination of the Cold War" is a misleading way to put the problem. What does it mean? The kind of cooperation and competition the United States now has with allies, where there are also degrees of common interest and divergence? With friendly neutrals? With countries neither really friendly nor hostile, like India and China? It is asking too much. In those terms the answer has to be bleak.

It is conceivable that the United States and the Soviet Union might become allies again in the face of what both perceived to be an overwhelming common threat. But not only is that unlikely; it surely would not be in conditions of peace. Otherwise, full accommodation is hardly imaginable short of drastic changes in the internal structure of the Soviet Union, which I think will come some day but well beyond the horizon. When China is cited as an example of accommodation, it is well to remember that this resulted not only from certain internal changes in China but also as a factor in the strategic hostility between the United States and the Soviet Union. If the Chinese experiment at home really works— and I think it may take a generation or more to have the answer— that will exert great pressure on the Soviet Union for a lot more internal changes than they are currently able to envisage, but it would not necessarily end the Cold War.

In saying that the big change will have to come within the Soviet Union, it should be remembered that Soviet relations with their own allies are primarily a function of force. It is self-deluding to think that equal changes within the United States are needed, or would make a big difference. The reason for relations based on force and ideology is that this is the source of legitimacy for the Soviet leadership. The kind of internal success that would provide a legitimacy based on consent (with or without our kind of elections) would of itself mean such a sea change in the Soviet structure of authority that it would constitute the drastic evolution I am talking about. Sooner or later, the Soviet Union will surely make such important steps, but it is not now foreseeable.

Nonetheless, this does not necessarily foreclose considerable improvement in Soviet-American relations, along with diminished arsenals. Security could be improved with less, though neither side could be expected to settle for less than security. The first crucial step, I think, is to identify common interests. It is a mistake to put this, as so often is done, in terms of "trust" or "sincerity."

There are a number of common interests already evident, and as they are more evidently acknowledged, others will emerge. The main ones are the prevention of large-scale nuclear war, the limitation of regional conflicts so that client states cannot drag in the superpowers, eventually environmental issues. I doubt that the Soviet Union can be brought into cooperative engagement on third world development problems for a long time. They are overwhelmingly concerned with their own development.

Management of the U.S.-Soviet relationship so as to reduce fear of war would certainly ease tensions and permit all kinds of subsidiary exchanges and activities which could be desirable and useful, but could not be expected to "terminate" the Cold War. It would also create some new problems as other countries see more room to maneuver within the East-West context and to assert their own interests. This would be true in both Eastern and Western Europe, and U.S.-Soviet relations would have to be supple enough to take this into account.

Both the United States and the Soviet Union have strong internal reasons to reduce their expenditures on arms, and both have strong internal pressures to continue them. This is a reciprocal process. Turning the spiral around does not depend on "trust" but on the difficult effort to reach agreements which each side considers at least as beneficial to itself as to the other. Each step taken will help open the way for the next step. But it is not practically helpful to seek some flight of the imagination or some great new spirit that will suddenly produce the happy day without plodding each bit of the way.

In short, there are a lot of reasons and possibilities for limiting the arms race and for improving relations. But the Soviet Union and the United States are likely to continue seeing each other as adversaries. That would already be much better.

# REV. THEODORE M. HESBURGH

President, University of Notre Dame

In responding to the question of whether or not I believe that a peaceful termination of the Cold War is a real possibility in the foreseeable future, I am sustained by the virtue of hope: I believe that the world will emerge from the Cold War, or else it will disappear in nuclear holocaust. The term Cold War describes quite clearly our present predicament, the recognition by all concerned that we and our adversaries are now *at war,* and have been so for almost four decades. A distinction is made between our present situation and a "shooting war," but we need to reflect on just how close we are, and have been, to the brink. The two superpowers have been building up their arsenals at a fantastic rate for over a generation, until now they have at their disposal the power to obliterate each other, and the rest of the world, ten times over.

Beyond arming themselves, and their allies and client states, they are constantly engaged in espionage, in electronic surveillance, in provocative war games and military exercises virtually on each other's borders, and in the most virulent and inflammatory rhetoric directed by their political leaders to their own constituents, and to all members of international society.

Modern technology has sharply reduced the time and space which forty years ago separated the antagonists, and provided for some margin of error on either side. Now the nuclear arsenals are not just buried in the earth, but are aimed very precisely at hundreds of targets within each country, and these enormous systems of offensive weapons, with a destructive potential that outreaches the human imagination, are literally on hair trigger: we are both literally just minutes away from annihilation and we cannot save ourselves; we can only try to guarantee that our foes will die with us.

And so, year in and year out, we brace ourselves in a posture of military readiness, with our forces on global alert, our safety dependent upon electronic eyes, ears, and brains—with all of their known fallibilities—while our global society is being twisted and corrupted by the preaching of hatred, by the diversion of desperately needed resources to the instruments of war, and by a technology of death that has become our master not our slave.

The so-called hawks on both sides talk about the imperative need for preparedness, and cite the example of World War II—of the Japanese surprise attack on Pearl Harbor and Hitler's surprise attack on the Soviet Union—as arguments for eternal armed vigilance. Those who press the argument of peace through strength say that if you want peace, prepare for war. But the real lesson of history is that if you want war, prepare for war. Rather than looking at the aberrations of World War II, we might consider the more instructive parallel case of the period in Europe immediately prior to World War I. During those early decades of the twentieth century no European nation was under direct attack by another, but all were preparing for war as fast as they could. They built armies and navies, developed treaties and alliances, and postured and strutted about, creating an explosive atmosphere which only needed a spark. And the spark appeared in the form of an absurd incident involving the assassination of a single man, the Archduke Ferdinand at Sarajevo. That single desperate act started a chain reaction which resulted in the almost total devastation of Europe and the slaughter of tens of millions of people—not because anyone wanted or planned for that to happen, but because their Cold War antics set the stage for an unspeakable tragedy. That is where the parallel with our own age and situation is so frighteningly clear: after forty years of effort, and trillions of dollars in expenditures for the implements of war, we find ourselves in a desperate situation, where the actions of a single madman, or the malfunction of a computer, could end civilization on earth.

When considering how we might extricate ourselves from this dilemma, we might consider that our Founding Fathers assumed that the infant United States was then, and would continue to be, at peace with all other nations, and if an unforeseen situation developed, or if a series of untoward incidents should occur, which seriously threatened to alter our relationship with another nation, it was left to the Congress to discuss the matter at length before coming to a decision as to whether or not we should declare a state of war existing between us and another people.

But now, as we have already noted, we have been for almost forty years in a state of war—Cold War—with the Soviet Union, and we seem unable to find any way out of our predicament, short of having our adversaries declare an unconditional surrender, an event as unlikely for one side as for the other. But while Congress, despite the Constitution, seems to have a diminishing role in establishing the quality of the relationship we shall enjoy with other nations, there is no reason why members of the House and Senate should not begin a public discussion of the terms and conditions under which we would be ready to move from a state of Cold War with the Soviet Union to a state of peace.

If we really began to discuss such matters in the clear light of day, what demands would we realistically place upon the Soviet Union as a precondition to the establishment of peaceful relations? And what might their reciprocal demands be? My guess is that after a period of jaw-boning, our non-negotiable demands would be relatively modest—and so would those of the Soviet Union—involving neither the demand for the abandonment of capitalism or communism, or the renunciation of Marxism or Christianity, or the unilateral disarmament of either side.

It seems to me that it might be a very rewarding and very educational project for U.S. people to begin such a discussion among themselves. We cannot realistically say that if our adversaries stop arming, or disarm, we will have peace. At first, we have to establish the firm possibility of peace; then we can both begin to disarm. We might never be able to get everyone in the United States, or in the Soviet Union, to agree on a set of minimum demands, but at the very least such a discussion is better from almost every point of view than the continued debate about how each is to achieve military domination of the other.

# BARBARA EPSTEIN

Associate Professor of History,
University of California, Santa Cruz

I take the term "Cold War" to mean not just rivalry between the United States and the Soviet Union but a state of acute antagonism between the two, involving an escalating nuclear arms race and an attempt to subordinate all political issues to this conflict. While it is quite conceivable that the rhetorical intensity of the Cold War might diminish, and President Reagan, or his successor, might make gestures toward arms control in an attempt to reassure the U.S. public, it seems unlikely that the actual antagonism between the two societies—or the military build-up that accompanies it— will end soon.

Antagonism between the United States and the Soviet Union has existed since the Bolshevik Revolution. It has been based upon the fact that the United States and the Soviet Union represent competing social systems, and on the fact that the land mass and geographical position of each nation has meant that by the time of the Bolshevik Revolution it was clear that both were on their way to becoming major world powers.

The antagonism between the United States and the Soviet Union was given particular intensity, however, after World War II. The United States emerged from that war stronger than any other nation in the world, and with the desire to translate that power into world domination. The Soviet Union, with its antagonism to capitalism and its own potential power, stood in the way of that desire. The Soviet Union has not been innocent of involvement in the Cold War, but the Soviet Union was not responsible for its inauguration, and it is unlikely that the Soviet Union could have reversed it. There have been moments when the United States has put aside the active pursuit of world power: in the wake of the Vietnam war, for instance, the United States refrained from active intervention in the third world and began to improve its relations with the Soviet Union. But as the Vietnam war receded into the past, it was possible for the right wing to revive the goal of world power, and with it the sharp antagonism to the Soviet Union of the immediate postwar years.

I do not think that there is anything inevitable about the U.S. pursuit of world power, or the anti-Sovietism that has accompanied it. In 1947 Henry Wallace argued that these policies did not represent the best interests of the United States; had the political climate of the time been different, he might have won the debate. In the mid-1970s, the Trilateral Commission, and Nixon and Kissinger, tried to fashion a foreign policy that did not require direct U.S. intervention in the third world, and that left room for somewhat improved relations with the Soviet Union. This policy was defeated by the worsening economic situation, and by the overthrow of U.S. surrogates in the third world—in particular the Shah of Iran—whose job it had been to make direct U.S. intervention unnecessary. But the reinstitution of U.S. interventionism, and anti-Sovietism, was not an inevitable response to these events. In a different political climate, the success of third world revolutions might have led the United States to reexamine the basic assumptions of its foreign policy.

While interventionism and acute anti-Sovietism are not inevitable components of U.S. foreign policy, both have become so intrinsic to U.S. political culture, over the last four decades, that it is very difficult to get rid of them. This is so in spite of the fact that both are now causing problems for the United States. In the 1950s, a militarized economy went with widespread prosperity; in the 1980s, the two are no longer so easily compatible. The arms race, which the Reagan administration hopes will destroy the Soviet economy before it bankrupts the United States, is a major factor in the fragility of the U.S.—and the international—economy. Reagan's early belligerent remarks about the Soviet Union frightened many people and threatened to undermine his popular support. While quick victories such as Grenada may be popular in the United States, any steps toward an intervention that would meet resistance—as in Nicaragua—arouses substantial popular protest. All of this leads the Reagan administration to move cautiously, but not to abandon its fundamental goals, to which it, and the conservative movement that it represents, are deeply committed.

In the 1950s it was very difficult for the left or the peace movement to challenge U.S. militarism, because at least for the moment the United States seemed to have so much to gain from it, and so little to lose. The fact that the costs of militarism have become more evident in the 1980s opens up the possibility of successful opposition. It seems to me that what stands in the way of the emergence of mass opposition is the fragile, uncertain state of the U.S. economy. Somehow, during the Reagan years, the economy has managed to stay more or less afloat: while the poor are suffering, many middle-class people are doing reasonably well. At the same time, there is widespread fear that real trouble, if not collapse, may come at any time. It is as if many people are collectively holding their breath, hoping that things do not get any worse. The same is true in relation to foreign policy: there is a widespread mood—shared by those in the Reagan administration—of wanting to avoid upsetting the applecart, hoping to maintain the current U.S. posture of international strength—or bravado—without having to pay the price of nuclear war.

A moment when political culture is dominated by the desire to hold onto what one has, and the fear that it might be taken away, is not a propitious time for the emergence of protest. The left and the peace movement can challenge the assumptions that underlie this mood. We can point out that the prosperity of the 1980s excludes many people and is based upon an attack on social welfare and humane values, and that the current relative international stability masks the most dangerous build-up of international tensions that the human race has ever experienced. While such arguments will win some people over, it seems to me that as long as the current fragile prosperity and fragile international stability are maintained, the peace movement is likely to be small and sporadic. If the economy were to actually grow and thrive, as it did in the 1960s, a certain kind of movement, based on altruism and idealism, would be possible. But this is not likely. If the economy should falter, and massive numbers of people should begin to experience the cost of spending for arms rather than human needs, a powerful anti-militarism could develop.

It seems to me that it is important to recognize that there are some moments that are simply not very propitious for the growth of protest movements, that there is a rhythm to the development of popular movements that is not subject to our control. Massive popular movements have arisen in the United States in cycles of roughly thirty years. If this cycle, which has held for more than a century, persists, we may expect another period of protest to begin by the early 1990s. This pattern is likely to be reinforced by the hardships that many people will probably be experiencing by that time: the effects of Reagan's domestic and foreign policies will no doubt be fully evident by then.

This is not to argue that we put aside politics until the next period of activism arrives. During the slow part of the cycle of U.S. protest, it is important to maintain the basic structures of left and peace movements, and to be receptive to new currents and new ideas that may provide the basis for an upsurge of protest. It is also important to understand that we cannot will a new surge of activism: it will come about in response to events, and political/cultural shifts, that cannot be predicted.

# MICHAEL MCCGWIRE

Senior Fellow in Foreign Policy Studies, Brookings Institution

What is this thing we call the "Cold War"? It is a manifestation of superpower rivalry, a competition not only between states but also between fundamentally different social systems. But beyond that is an animus on our side that plays a major role in turning rivalry into "war." This unilateral aspect of the problem is reflected in the way we define the competition in moral terms, as a struggle between good and evil, freedom and slavery. The Soviet Union defines it in evolutionary terms, as a struggle between an outmoded system of capitalist-imperialism and the emerging system of world socialism.

Peaceful termination of the Cold War requires that both aspects of the problem be resolved, and it will be seen that the psychological (subjective) one is the most intractable. Although the structural (objective) aspect of the problem is inherently complex, if we are willing to recognize certain asymmetries and similarities in the perceptions and interests of the two superpowers, we will also have identified the way out of this impasse.

One of these asymmetries concerns the way the two sides perceive the danger that faces them. In the period 1948–1953, the Soviet Union and the West both assumed the other was preparing for military invasion. Thereafter, Soviet perceptions evolved and by 1959 the threat of a premeditated Western attack had been discounted. This did not, however, remove the danger of world war, which remained inherent in the antagonisms of the two social systems. Western perceptions of a threat, meanwhile, did not evolve. By 1953 they had become encased in deterrence theory, which was premised on a Soviet urge to invade Europe—an assumption that was further reinforced by NATO's military bureaucracy, whose existence it justified. This means that in Moscow, the primary danger is seen as unintended global war, whereas in Washington, the danger is Soviet aggression which, if not deterred, would lead to war. The Western viewpoint is shaped by Munich, the Soviet one by Sarajevo.

A second critical asymmetry is geostrategic. Although one of the Soviet Union's primary objectives is to avoid world war, it must cover the contingency of its becoming inescapable. If the Soviet Union is not to lose such a war, it must defeat NATO in Europe, evict U.S. forces from the continent, and prevent them from returning. If the United States is not to lose, all it needs to do is check the Soviet offensive before the bridgehead in Europe is lost. To have a reasonable chance that its offensive will not be checked by NATO, Soviet forces require a margin of superiority that is sufficient to overcome the advantage of defense. This means that the Warsaw Pact forces facing NATO have an inherently offensive posture, while NATO is inherently defensive. This offensive posture does not reflect some urge to acquire Europe (which can be deterred), but a strategic imperative that would be triggered by the portentous decision that war is inescapable.

A third major asymmetry concerns the superpowers' interest in strategic arms control. Having achieved strategic superiority in World War II, the United States naturally sought to preserve that advantage. From the time of the Baruch Plan, arms control negotiations have been used (in practice, if not in theory) as a way of capping and, if possible, reducing Soviet inventories in areas where the Soviet Union was catching up or moving ahead, while excluding other areas where asymmetries in force structure and/or advanced technology would allow the United States to retain an advantage.

The Soviet Union, meanwhile, has sought to use arms control as an alternative to arms racing in order to deny the United States its strategic superiority. The doctrinal decision in late 1966 that, if war came, it might be possible to avoid escalation to an intercontinental exchange meant that strategic superiority was no longer a Soviet military requirement. This theoretical acceptance of parity as an objective was reinforced by practical considerations. If the United

States had been unable to retain its advantage over the technologically backward Soviet Union, what chance did the latter have of achieving superiority over the former?

Since the late 1960s, the Soviet Union has seen arms control as being very much in its interest, whereas the United States has always been of two minds about its merits. Even those in the United States who favor negotiations do so for somewhat different reasons than those in the Soviet Union. Both parties consider that successful agreements improve the prospects for peace. But while the Soviets see arms control as a political process which makes war less likely by halting the arms race and reducing international tensions, U.S. arms controllers are more concerned with the technical and theoretical issues of stable deterrence and crisis stability. The Soviet Union believes in the traditional approach of trying to avoid creating situations that could lead to war, and it does not welcome crises. The United States focuses on preventing war by deterring the temptation in a crisis to launch a preemptive attack and, because it thinks it can thereby control events, its attitude is more ambivalent. The concept of crisis management and terms like brinkmanship imply that crises can work to U.S. advantage.

The perceptual problem created by these asymmetries is compounded by the effects of action-reaction (which means that procurement cycles are out of phase), and also by the different levels of technological capability. The United States has been able to make large technological leaps and then rely on relatively minor structural modifications to greatly improve the original capability of its deployed weapons systems. The Soviet Union has had to rely on the slow and expensive process of product improvement, with a replacement program following close on the heels of its predecessor, an approach that invites characterization as a "relentless build-up." In fact, the Soviet Union is very much the tortoise and the United States the hare. In the case of intercontinental missiles, it took the Soviet Union the best part of fifteen years to draw near the massive U.S. capability, which was initially deployed in the first half of the 1960s.

Western concern over the build-up of Soviet conventional forces during the 1970s was better founded, and there is no doubt that the

Soviet Union was seeking the capability for a successful offensive in Europe, should war be inescapable. This was not, however, a new objective. What we saw in the 1970s was a restructuring of Soviet forces in Europe to give them the capability for preventive attacks against NATO's nuclear delivery systems and command structure, and for a massive blitzkrieg offensive striking deep in the rear, all this using conventional means only. This operational concept, which stemmed from the doctrinal decision in late 1966, sought to inhibit NATO's resort to nuclear weapons in the theater and hence make escalation to an intercontinental exchange less likely. The concept was made feasible by NATO's adoption of "flexible response," and the strategic imperative meant that this opening had to be exploited, despite the adverse effects on détente. Similarly, the build-up of forces along the Chinese border (where the Soviet Union is defensively postured) largely reflects this new requirement to rely on conventional rather than nuclear weapons, for fear of precipitating escalation.

The fourth major asymmetry is very different and concerns the way the two sides view the world at large, although the similarities in this area are really more striking than the disparities. For example, in its relationship to the developing world, the United States sees itself as the legitimate custodian of the legacy of worldwide influence and attitudes from the West's colonial past, while the Soviet Union sees these same remnants of European empire as natural adherents to what it envisages as an emerging social system.

Moving closer to home, both superpowers implicitly think and act in terms of a national security zone. This is a somewhat fluid concept, but, as with the idea of social or economic security, the greater one's wealth and power, the more extensive one's definition of security. Since the mid-1950s, the Soviet Union's primary national security zone has encompassed Finland, the Warsaw Pact nations, Afghanistan, Mongolia, and now may include northern Iran. The United States' primary national security zone is much longer established and encompasses the entire American continent north of the equator. Each superpower considers that it has a vital interest in the political orientation and allegiance of the states in its zone and, if its security interests clash with the preferences of the individual states, the interests of the metropolitan power prevail. Furthermore, the ratchet effect of the search for security means that both superpowers resist any attempt by states in their zone to move in the direction of a more distant relationship, whether from closely aligned to neutrality, or from neutrality to enmity.

The two sides use different means to maintain control of their national security zones, differences that reflect geostrategic circumstances as well as political systems. The practical effects in terms of the social welfare of the majority of each population outside the metropolitan state are, however, not all that different. A horticultural analogy may clarify this assessment. The Soviet Union, a harsh land lying north of 50°N, has traditionally concentrated on growing vegetables in orderly rows, and it has applied this same approach to the adjoining land of its national security zone. The United States, a bountiful land between 30° and 50°N, has chosen open parkland, which is obviously much preferable to serried rows of vegetables. But parkland is expensive to maintain; hence the land in the U.S. national security zone has been largely neglected, apart from periodic forays to destroy noxious weeds and pests that were seen to endanger the home estate. In other words, a peasant's life in Hungary or Poland could well be preferable to one in El Salvador or Guatemala.

It is only when we turn to the superpowers' views of their place in the broader sweep of history that the asymmetry in world view really emerges. Each state sees itself as being at a late stage of some process of sociopolitical evolution. The Soviet Union claims explicitly that it represents the penultimate stage of a historical process, the final stage being the withering away of the state, leaving a communist society. Comparable claims are implicit in the U.S. concept of manifest destiny and the crusading belief in the virtues of the U.S. political economy. The critical difference between the two perceptions is that the Soviet Union considers that it must evolve through a further stage before it reaches the final goal, whereas the United States believes that, except for running adjustments, it has already reached the objective.

The perception of where one stands on the ladder of history affects how one views the flow of world events. The Soviet Union defines the status quo as an inevitable evolutionary process that can be checked but not stopped (except by global nuclear war), while the United States defines it as static and something to be preserved. If one sees oneself as being on the side of inevitable progress (as does the Soviet Union), a long-term perspective is in order and one accepts that one can afford to win some–lose some in the competition for world influence. If, however, one is concerned to protect one's favored position from encroachment (as is the West in general and the United States in particular), every challenge must be repulsed.

This, of course, has implications for how one sees the role of military force in distant parts of the world. For the Soviet Union, its primary role is to protect fledgling socialist regimes from attempts by anti-progressive forces (usually defined as the Western powers) to overthrow them. For the West, the primary role of military force is to preserve order in the international system, where order and the status quo are often seen as synonymous. The result has been that Soviet military intervention (outside its national security zone) has invariably been "supportive," whereas U.S. intervention has frequently been "coercive." And while the Soviet Union's use of supportive force has invariably been "protective" (e.g., air defense), the United States' use has often been "punitive" (e.g., shelling Druse villages or bombing Hanoi).

Contributing to these differing views of the political utility of coercive force are the asymmetries that were discussed earlier. The Sarajevo model, the belief that wars are avoided rather than prevented, and the sensitivity to nuclear escalation all tend to restrain policies that might lead to superpower confrontation in the third world. The Munich model, and the belief that crises can be controlled and war prevented by the threat of escalation, reinforce the tendency to turn to military force as a first, rather than a last, resort.

There are also historical reasons for this disparity. U.S. attitudes toward the role of projected force have their roots in the European experience of maritime colonialism, founded on naval power. These attitudes were reinforced by World War II, when the success of its arms brought the United States fully onto the world scene, and it was the predominance of military and economic power that allowed the United States to shape the postwar world, albeit benevolently, but still in its own interests. The Soviet Union, meanwhile, had the tsarist experience of continental expansion and a reluctance to take (or retain) possession of distant territories, while their own experience of World War II centered on the ejection and military defeat of the German invaders.

But the main difference with the West lies in the fact of the Russian Revolution, when the new state consciously sought to cast off the outdated ideas and attitudes of capitalist imperialism and introduce new approaches founded on Marxism. Central to Marxist theory was the idea that it is socioeconomic forces that shape history. Military power would be required to counter attempts by the ruling classes to suppress these forces, but the revolution would not be spread on the swords of a socialist jihad. Socioeconomic forces and historical inevitability would between them change the world.

Paradoxically, it is this central belief of Marxist theory that offers a way of addressing the objective aspects of the problem that faces us, and of moving from a state of Cold War to what Marshall Shulman has called an "adversary relationship" and what the Soviets refer to as "peaceful coexistence."

The key lies in the economic axiom that a nation will maximize its welfare by pursuing its comparative advantage. When we consider the two social systems, we see that the United States has considerable advantages in the socioeconomic field. Its economic instruments of foreign policy are potentially much stronger than those of the Soviet Union. Its political system can provide a generally high standard of living for its people, combined with broad political participation, something that the Soviet Union has been unable to achieve. And its political ideology favors the individual over the state, while Communism favors the reverse. The United States also has inherent advantages in the matter of physical security. It is predominant in its own hemisphere, which is remote from the rest of the world, whereas the Soviet Union has traditional enemies on most sides and does not enjoy military predominance. The U.S. homeland can only be severely threatened by intercontinental nuclear systems, whereas the Soviet Union's vulnerability to all forms of attack has been demonstrated over the centuries.

The one area where the United States is at a significant geographic disadvantage is in the projection of military force. The Soviet Union is Mackinderland, sprawled across 170° of longitude, looking south on half the world. Over 80 percent of the world's population lies within three thousand miles (air lift range) of the Soviet Union's borders, and the more interesting parts are within two thousand miles. In contrast, the United States is Mahanland, remote from the rest of the world. To make matters worse, the cost of projecting military force at a distance has been rising exponentially, while its political utility has been steadily diminishing.

The principle of comparative advantage argues that the United States should welcome the Soviet Union's choice of a socioeconomic arena for the struggle between the two systems, and should reduce its emphasis on military instruments of policy such as nuclear deterrence, physical containment, and coercive intervention. Shifting the struggle to the socioeconomic arena would also have a beneficial effect on the other asymmetries. It would tacitly acknowledge that the common danger was war, from whatever source. By lessening the chances of military confrontation in the third world, it would have the effect of moving the United States in the direction of working to avoid crisis situations rather than seeking to control them. And a long-term improvement in the climate of international relations would reduce the danger of war and make it easier for the Soviet Union to accept parity in the number of forces facing each other in Europe.

Objectively, the dictates of comparative advantage are compelling, both as regards U.S. economic interests and the broader interests of avoiding nuclear war, and if that were the whole problem we might move to its resolution. It is here that the real difficulties lie, and the evidence suggests that the majority of the U.S. people do not want a real accommodation with the Soviet Union; nor do they see any compelling need to reach one. The reasons for this attitude, which goes back to the earliest days of the Soviet state, are manifold and there is no room to analyze them here. Some of the reasons are well founded, while others use the Soviet Union or Communism as a scapegoat for various ills. It is important, however, to realize that this U.S. attitude is not shared by either the Soviet people, or (at least until recently) by their government.

From its earliest days, the Soviet Union has persistently sought a measure of accommodation with the United States. This was largely for reasons of narrow self-interest, but it was also because both the people and their leadership harbored a genuine respect and often an admiration for the United States and many of its attributes. For example, it was Stalin who, through June 1947, held onto the hope that elements of the collaborative wartime relationship would endure, although the Anglo-Saxon powers had decided in the Spring of 1946 that Soviet behavior was such as to preclude the possibility of normal relations. Similarly, it was the Soviet Union that persisted through early 1983 in the claim that détente was irreversible, while the United States had decided by 1978–1979 that the relationship was no longer tenable.

Americans do not respect the Soviet Union and they abhor its political system. There are good reasons for this, but that does not mean that our approach has to be that of a magistrate toward a lawbreaker, rather than that of an entrepreneur toward a very tough competitor. This is a hard point to get across to the U.S. people, and a change of attitude may have to wait on a build-up of economic constraints that will force us to reduce our reliance on military instruments of policy and concentrate our efforts in the socioeconomic arena.

By then, of course, it may be too late and the venue may have been changed. It would not surprise me if, on the basis of U.S. policy in the 1978–1983 period, the Soviet Union has concluded that the struggle will have to be waged primarily in the political-military arena.

# GIL GREEN

Author, *Cold War Fugitive*

Yes, the Cold War can be terminated peacefully. What other alternative is there if the arms race is to be halted and the threat of nuclear war banished?

Ending the Cold War does not require that the contending powers love each other. It could give way to a cold or cool peace, with mutual recognition that whatever tensions exist now, or arise tomorrow, must be resolved peacefully.

Once this premise is accepted unconditionally, options will arise for mutually beneficial cooperation—extension of trade, scientific and cultural exchange, interplanetary exploration, protection of the earth's ecosystem, ending world hunger, and building a lasting peace.

Yet there is no assurance at this time that the Cold War will be ended. New factors offer hope for change, but must first be resolved in the interests of peace. I shall comment on a few:

*1. The survival factor.* It is now generally acknowledged that a nuclear war cannot be won and could extinguish life on earth. This is so overriding a concern as would normally suffice to preserve peace. Although the Cold War involves an abnormal, not a normal, state of mind, the recognition that both powers must coexist or not exist at all should in time be decisive in determining their relationship.

The Reagan administration has recently altered its former public position that a protracted nuclear war was winnable. It now asserts the opposite. This is a hopeful change. Unfortunately, events since then raise doubts of how committed Reagan is to this newer perception.

Washington still opposes a nuclear freeze, rejects Moscow's proposals to ban all nuclear testing, with the right of on-site verification, and has no meaningful proposals of its own to slow down or reverse the arms race. Instead, it recklessly pushes its Star Wars stratagem, aimed at filling the heavens with nuclear-triggered anti-ballistic missiles. Through perfecting a Sky Wars technology, the administration is gambling on attaining a first-strike capability while blunting an effective retaliatory response.

Hence the administration still clings to the belief that a nuclear war can be won with the aid of new technological gimmickry. This is sheer madness. Any attempt of either power to gain military mastery over the other can only further unsettle world relations and heighten the danger of nuclear war—by accident, miscalculation, or design.

2. *The economic factor*. The endless waste of huge national resources on the military is gradually impoverishing the nation, undermining its basic infrastructure and industrial capability, and feeding the Pentagon at the expense of essential human needs.

Despite superficial appearances to the contrary (the huge profits of the arms manufacturers, the rash of nonproductive corporate takeovers—often with junk bonds as collateral—the repeated waves of stock market speculation), our economy is heading for trouble. Preeminent in world markets only a few decades ago, we now face a yearly foreign trade deficit of $150 billion.

Corporate profits are being spent less on the renewal of plant capacity at home and more on the export of capital and jobs to lands where wages are much lower and specific technologies higher. In addition, our federal yearly deficit has jumped from $58 billion in 1981 to over $200 billion for 1985. The only purpose of the administration's rhetoric about balancing the budget has been to slash spending on vital social needs while spending for the military soared.

Draconian measures now employed for balancing the budget aim at still more cuts in spending for health, housing, education, mass transit, and the elderly, with the aim of shifting all such programs from the federal to state and local governments.

How long can this continue? What will happen when the next cyclical depression strikes, with many more millions of jobless, a sharp drop in mass purchasing power, and reduced revenues for government? The outlook is for a social crisis of major dimensions.

3. *The third world factor.* The eminent British scientist J. D. Bernal once wrote that the most expensive operation in the world is the preservation of poverty. The resources spent yearly on the military, he explained, could provide a high standard of life for every person on earth within a generation.

This is something to ponder in face of the United States' homeless and the millions in dire need. But it is a hundred times worse for the peoples of the third world. Yet it is not the only way in which the arms race affects them. The Cold War provides a pretext for intervening against governments not to "our" liking. Nor does it matter whether the government set up for slaughter is democratically elected or brought to office by revolutionary means, as was our own republic in 1776. The Arbenz government in Guatemala, overthrown in 1954, and the Allende government in Chile, overthrown in 1973, were both democratically elected.

Our country intervened in the internal affairs of Latin America long before there was a Cold War. We robbed Mexico of its richest lands more than a century ago, turned Puerto Rico into our colony at the turn of the century, and U.S. Marines occupied Nicaragua years before there was a Russian Revolution.

Now that we claim vital national interests all over the globe, our interventions have become global. About three thousand military bases and installations are located on foreign soil, many of them in third world countries, thereby drawing them directly into the Cold War.

The unequal conditions of world trade to which these countries are subjected, and the stagnation in the world capitalist market these past years, have put most third world countries in an economic noose. They lack foreign exchange with which to buy essential needs abroad or to make payment on the huge loans borrowed from Western banks in years when the world market was expanding. Most of these countries cannot even meet the yearly interest and service charges on their debt. This is creating a major crisis. The International Monetary Fund, acting for the Western banks, presses for ever greater belt tightening. This has brought vast popular unrest and the toppling of some of the most brutal military dictatorships. The newly elected government in Peru has declared that it will spend no more than 10 percent of its yearly foreign earnings on its debt. It is a sign of the times.

How will Washington react to this crisis? If it blames Moscow or Havana it will only make matters worse. In face of the mass upheavals in Haiti and the Philippines, Washington decided to accept the inevitable for the time being, so long as U.S. military bases and corporate interests remain untouched. It hopes that the changes will only be cosmetic.

But the peoples of the third world yearn for *real* change, for an end to harrowing poverty, illiteracy, and disease, and for a better life for their children.

The Reagan administration's actions toward Nicaragua and Angola, its overthrow of the government of Grenada, its refusal to end the economic blockade of Cuba, its duplicitous support of the apartheid regime in South Africa—all these offer little hope of any meaningful change in Washington's policies toward the third world in the period immediately ahead.

4. *The key factor—the movement for change.* Important differences over policies exist in U.S. ruling-class circles, and even within the Reagan administration itself. These will multiply as the dead-end nature of current policies become more evident. At this juncture, however, they surface only intermittently and then submerge, in the name of unity, behind the President. Reagan's reelection reinforced the belief that the country is on his side and that opposition is futile. This explains, but only in part, the craven capitulation of most Democratic Party leaders and liberals in Congress to the blandishments and pressures of the White House. This may change as the crisis over policy deepens and the President is seen as more of a lame duck.

Differences in top circles cannot, however, bring the changes needed to end the Cold War. Corporate interests have a stake in continuing high profits from military production and research and in Reagan's reactionary domestic policies and union busting. Differences at the top can only assume critical importance if a powerful movement for meaningful change emerges.

The potential for such exists. The U.S. people fear nuclear war and want peace. This was shown in hundreds of local and state referendums on the issue of a nuclear freeze. Of great importance is the existence of an influential network of peace committees and organizations.

The movement for peace has taken on considerable breadth, including the most important religious denominations. These challenge the very existence of nuclear weapons. A larger sector of the labor movement is also involved in peace efforts, particularly around the crisis in Central America and South Africa. In addition, there is the movement of black people, in their churches and community organizations, with their most prestigious national leaders as spokepersons. Hispanic organizations and movements are likewise extremely active and growing. The women's movement is also definitely on the side of peace and progress, and there are signs of a renewed commitment and activism on the campuses, with impressive and militant demonstrations in support of the South African and Nicaraguan people.

Thus the potential movement for change is infinitely greater than the organized peace movement per se. As every increase in military spending comes from robbing people of gains won over decades, every form of resistance to this is part of the movement for meaningful change. This may not always be evident to activists battling on different fronts, but the way to fulfill the promise of a powerful united movement lies precisely in establishing a common identity and solidarity.

One reason for the inability of the peace movement to take the offensive against Reagan's militarist and reactionary policies is the inhibiting effects of anti-Sovietism and anti-Communism. On the one hand we are warned that the Soviet system is a failure and growing ever weaker, but on the other that it is so all-powerful, so much ahead of us militarily, that we must spend more and ever more to defend ourselves and every corner of the globe from the ogre-like Russians.

Intimidated by the pervasive anti-Sovietism, the peace movement has tended to blame both superpowers equally. This has made it impossible to place the main responsibility where it belongs. One may dislike the Soviet system and its government, but in the face of the most recent evidence it is clear that Soviet proposals have aimed at ending the arms race, while those of

Washington have done the opposite. It is not a question of choosing between the United States and the Soviet Union, but of supporting every *real* step to end the nuclear nightmare, no matter from where it comes.

The universality of the threat of nuclear annihilation makes possible an ecumenical movement inclusive of every person or group desirous of peace, irrespective of other differences. It also calls for great perseverance and dedication. Varied types of peace formations are possible wherever people are found—in neighborhoods, campuses, churches, work places, and trade unions. As was true during the Vietnam war, these can become ever more visible and audible, reacting to every new threat and flooding the White House and Congress with protests and Washington with massive demonstrations. It was in this way that the nation made its will felt during the Vietnam war, compelling war hawks like Nixon and Kissinger to sue for peace.

The movement can also find expression during the election campaign, placing every candidate squarely on record, not hesitating to field independent candidates in party primaries or on independent lines. The time has come to refuse to go along with wishy-washy liberals who say one thing to get elected and then betray their promises once in office.

The hope of ending the Cold War and arms race lies precisely in such a development. From it could emerge a new political alliance that can in time change the course of the nation.

# MANNING MARABLE

Professor of Sociology and Political Science, Purdue University;
columnist, *In These Times*

The worldwide confrontation between the United States and the Soviet Union, which is expressed most sharply in the proliferation of nuclear weapons, is the central geopolitical fact of the second half of the twentieth century. If this situation of Cold War instability and conflict remains for several more decades, into the twenty-first century, it is probable that human civilization as we know it will be destroyed.

Yet nuclear war is avoidable. The Cold War can be resolved through a series of peaceful negotiations between the superpowers. But this can only occur if the advocates of peace are able to challenge the basic political assumptions and special interests which perpetuate the policies of confrontation and nuclear escalation.

The U.S. people are bombarded daily by the media and most elected officials with propaganda which rationalizes the Cold War, and the dire necessity to spend billions of dollars on conventional and nuclear weapons. Frequently, the electorate supports those candidates who are most bellicose on the subject of Soviet expansionism. President Reagan, after all, received 66 percent of the white electorate's support in 1984; he also won 68 percent of the votes of those who have incomes above $50,000 annually, and 80% of the votes of all "born-again" Christians. But the far right, despite its recent electoral triumphs, has failed to create a political consensus for nuclear war against the Soviet Union. According to the research of Daniel Yankelovich and John Doble, recent public opinion polls continue to show a strong desire for peace. "By an overwhelming 96 to 3 percent, Americans assert that 'picking a

120

fight with the Soviet Union is too dangerous in a nuclear world. . . .'
By 89 percent to 9 percent," Yankelovich and Doble note, "Americans subscribe to the view that 'there can be no winner in an all-out
nuclear war; both the United States and the Soviet Union would be
completely destroyed.' "

It is interesting to note that the segment of the public which is
most critical of the Cold War and the arms race is the black
community. In opinion polls, blacks consistently favor a nuclear
freeze by more than a 9 to 1 margin. Black U.S. Representatives in
Congress have repeatedly proposed the elimination of 20 to 30
percent of the Pentagon's total budget; and about 90 percent of all
blacks voted against Reagan in 1984. The challenge for progres-
sive politics in the United States, and the hope for world peace, is to
expand the political perspective of black Americans to embrace a
majority of the electorate.

Why is the political culture of white America so inclined to
accept the rhetoric and policies of the Cold War, and why are black
Americans less likely to do so? Part of the reason resides in the fear
and hatred of Communism, which is embedded deeply in the
popular discourse. Even among some black progressives and many
liberal reformers, a kind of crude caricature of Communism is
regularly projected. One example is provided by Martin Luther
King, Jr., who explained his firm opposition to Communism in his
1963 book, *Strength to Love*. "Communism and Christianity are
fundamentally incompatible," King observed. "A true Christian
cannot be a true Communist, for the two philosophies are antitheti-
cal and all the dialectics of the logicians cannot reconcile them."
For King, life under Communism "stripped" human beings of
"both conscience and reason. . . . Man has no inalienable rights.
Art, religion, education, music, and science come under the grip-
ping yoke of governmental control. Man must be a dutiful servant
to the omnipotent state."

The atrocities committed in the name of revolutionary Marxism,
from the gulags of Stalin to the irrational mass executions of the
Pol Pot regime in Kampuchea, have provided some of the ideological basis for militant anti-Communism in the United States. But
black Americans tend to perceive that such criticism of authoritarian regimes is distinctly one-sided. Chile, South Korea, Haiti, El

Salvador, the Philippines, and other pro-U.S. dictatorships which systematically oppress millions of people are not condemned as harshly as the Polish military's suppression of the Solidarity movement. Probably no nation in the entire world is more militantly anti-Communist than the apartheid regime in South Africa. But black Americans, and African people generally, recognize that South Africa is also a quasi-fascist state in which thousands of men and women are held in indefinite detention without charges or fair trial; where 3 million African children below the age of fifteen currently suffer from malnutrition; and where the prison population is the highest per capita in the entire world. The sterile polemics of anti-Communism frequently become the justification for brutalities and an abrogation of human rights that exceeds anything witnessed under most "Marxist states."

The ordeals of slavery, sharecropping, and legal Jim Crow provided black America with a special insight into the contradictions and inconsistencies of U.S. democracy. Only through massive nonviolent demonstrations, boycotts, legal suits, and the sacrificing of hundreds of lives were we permitted a modest measure of political and economic democracy, whether inside of this country or anywhere else in the world. The Westminster model of parliamentary government, or the U.S. system, represent only two flawed possibilities. The Cuban system of "people's power" includes municipal and neighborhood elections, based on a secret and direct ballot, with between two and eight Communist and non-Communist candidates for each seat. The mass constituency assemblies, women's and working people's formations created by the Grenada revolution provide another type of noncapitalist democratic process. Political dialogue between Marxists and non-Marxists can be productive for both sides. Problems in regulating the economy, preserving natural resources, and developing new methods of production often transcend narrow ideological boundaries. As Marxist states experiment with new forms of economic pluralism—China provides only one recent example—the West can learn from their practical experiences. Social systems are always in some stage of transition, and Western capitalist democracies certainly have not evolved to their final form.

A more dangerous factor in the pervasiveness of Cold War

political culture in the West is what I would term anti-Sovietism. In 1978, I was a Rockefeller Foundation fellow at Aspen Institute. General Edward Rowney, later to become President Reagan's chief arms negotiator, was a participant in my seminar. One day, quite accidently, the two of us were discussing Eurocommunism and the political implications of the breakdown in the monolithic Communist movement in Europe. Rowney assured me paternalistically that meaningful negotiations with Communists, and especially the Soviet Union, were almost impossible. "The Russians never experienced the Renaissance," the general observed. "They did not take part of Western culture." I inquired whether serious discussions leading to the reduction of the arms race were negated by the Soviet Union's adherence to Communism. "Communism has nothing to do with it," Rowney curtly replied. The real problem with the Soviet Union is that "they are Asiatics." President Reagan and his key advisers constantly echo Rowney's racial chauvinism when they describe the Soviet Union as an "evil empire." To perceive one's ideological adversary in such rigid, Faustian terms effectively voids any possibilities for sustained, constructive exchanges.

The proponents of peace and nuclear disarmament must overturn the demonology of anti-Sovietism among Americans. This does not mean the acceptance of every Soviet position regarding arms control, or the acquiescence to Soviet behavior or policies in Afghanistan or Poland. It does require the fundamental recognition of the reality and relative permanence of Soviet socialism, and an understanding that its people fervently desire peace. Cultural and educational exchanges between the American and Soviet people, if coordinated on a truly large scale, could begin to erode decades of anti-Soviet propaganda and hatred. Dialogues between U.S. Christian and Jewish groups with Soviet religious leaders, could provide tangible evidence that all Communists are not atheists. Working discussions between urban planners, trade unionists, artists, and representatives of other professions might form the foundation of greater political tolerance and understanding.

Black Americans also comprehend that peace is not the absence of conflict. As long as institutional racism, apartheid, and social class inequality exists, social tensions will erupt into confrontations. Most blacks recognize that peace is the realization of social justice and human dignity for all nations and historically oppressed peoples. Peace more than anything else is the recognition of the oneness of humanity. As Paul Robeson, the great black artist and activist, observed in his autobiographical work *Here I Stand,* "I learned that the essential character of a nation is determined not by the upper classes, but by the common people, and that the common people of all nations are truly brothers in the great family of mankind." Any people who experience generations of oppression gain an awareness of the innate commonality of all human beings, despite their religious, ethnic, and political differences. In order to reverse the logic of the Cold War, white Americans must begin to view themselves as a distinct minority in a world dominated by people of color. Peace between the superpowers is directly linked to the evolution of democratic rights, economic development, and social justice in the third world periphery.

Black intellectuals, from W.E.B. Du Bois to the present, have also comprehended their unique role in the struggle for peace and social justice. Cultural and intellectual activity for us is inseparable from politics. All art and aesthetics, scientific inquiry, and social studies are directly or indirectly linked to the material conditions of human beings, and the existing set of power relationships which dictate the policies of the modern state. When the intellectual and artist fail to combat racial or gender inequality, or the virus of anti-Semitism, their creative energies may indirectly contribute to the ideological justification for prejudice and social oppression. This is equally the case for the problem of war and peace. Through the bifurcation of our moral and social consciences against the cold abstractions of research and "value-free" social science, we may console ourselves by suggesting that we play no role in the escalation of the Cold War political culture. By hesitating to dedicate ourselves and our work to the pursuit of peace and social justice, we inevitably contribute to the dynamics of national chauvinism, militarism, and perhaps set the ideological basis necessary for World War III. Paul Robeson, during the Spanish Civil War, expressed the perspective of the black peace tradition as a passionate belief in humanity: "Every artist, every scientist must decide, now, where he stands. He has no alternative. There are no impartial observers . . ."

The commitment to contest public dogmas, the recognition that we share with the Soviet people a community of social, economic, and cultural interests, forces the intellectual into the terrain of ideological debate. If we fail to do so, and if the peace consensus of black America remains isolated from the electoral mainstream, the results may be the termination of humanity itself.

# MALCOLM W. GORDON

Adjunct Professor of Biochemistry, University of New Mexico

*[This response is excerpted from a lecture on Central America presented at the Newman Society, Albuquerque, New Mexico]*

At the end of World War II, policymakers both in the United States and in the Soviet Union contemplated the future with optimism. The United States emerged from the war the greatest military and economic power on earth, a fact underlined by our monopoly of the atom bomb. *Time* magazine, reflecting the outlook of leading U.S. policymakers, saw no force that could prevent our economic and political dominance of the world. *Time* hailed the beginning of what it called the "American century."

The Soviet Union saw a very different future. Despite the devastation of the Soviet Union by the war, its influence was widespread. Its leading role in the defeat of Hitler lent it unparalleled prestige. Soviet leaders envisaged the spread of socialism throughout the world, particularly in those countries that had been the colonies of the imperial powers.[. . .]

The forty years since World War II have exploded both these appraisals of the future. The atomic monopoly was broken. An inconclusive war was fought in Korea. Socialist forces won in Vietnam, but at the expense of China's defection from the Soviet bloc. Cuba became a socialist country, but the CIA masterminded the overthrow of left-oriented governments in Chile, Guatemala, and Indonesia. Israel, which gained its independence with Soviet bloc support, became the leading ally of the United States in the Near East. In Africa, the alliance of governments switched from socialist to capitalist and vice versa. In the Near East it is often difficult to say who can be counted a friend and who an enemy of either of the superpowers. Through it all there has been a steady deterioration in the life of the people of the third world, in growing contrast to the revival of the economies of Western Europe and Japan.

While attention was focused on the inconclusive contest between the superpowers, a new force was developing. A conference was held in Yugoslavia, attended by leaders of twenty-five countries, on September 16, 1961—the first meeting of the Movement of Non-Aligned Nations. Its foreign policy is "peaceful coexistence, equal state relations, cooperation for development, and an end to colonialism." It opposes the Cold War, supports anti-colonial struggles, and has taken sides in disputes between the developed and developing worlds. Over one hundred countries, including Nicaragua, now consider themselves part of the movement, nations comprising by far the majority of the world's population.

Some of these countries have socialist economies, others mixed ones; some have reverted to old religious fanaticism. Whatever their domestic orientation, however, their goal is national revival, a goal that they pursue without becoming clients of either superpower. They have exploded the myth of the zero-sum game. If a government develops close relations with the United States, it does not necessarily mean that the Soviet Union has a new enemy. And if a nation holds the United States at arms length, it does not mean that the Soviet Union has a new ally.

Even the words "capitalism" and "socialism" have not retained their old meaning in the third world. Experiments with socialist forms of government differ widely from the Soviet model. In Nicaragua almost none of the elements that comprise Lenin's concept of democratic centralism or a vanguard party have been followed. Instead, political parties of very different orientations contest for power in free elections. A strong alliance has been established between the government and elements of the Catholic church, in stark contrast to Poland. Even the economy is pluralistic, with 60 percent of agriculture and industry in private hands. In China, Yugoslavia, even in the Soviet bloc country of Hungary, major departures from the Soviet model are evident. And so with capitalism. In India, a country where private ownership of the means of production is widespread, elements of socialism are present and even encouraged in major segments of the economy. As old economic categories become blurred, so does the assumption that the foreign policy of a nation can be inferred from its social structure.

By the end of the war in Vietnam there were those both in the United States and the Soviet Union who recognized that the Cold War was a failure, that the contest would not be won on the terms originally envisioned. A period of détente ensued. Both governments edged toward accommodation as they saw that they would somehow have to live with one another, that total victory was not only an illusion, but its pursuit carried dangers of mutual annihilation. Not that the Nixon-Kissinger doctrine abandoned containment as the ground rock of U.S. policy; but it did shift away from the perimeter defense, the Kennedy plan to build an iron curtain around the entire Soviet bloc. Nixon downplayed ideological conflict and appealed to the nationalism of the Soviet Union through diplomatic, economic, and political pressure. The world was to be divided into mutually understood spheres of interest, within which each side would effectively agree to contain itself. Accordingly, Nixon officially ended World War II, recognized East Germany, worked out an agreement on Berlin, and accepted the de facto boundaries of Eastern Europe.

Kissinger now became anathema to the ultra-right, his services in the overthrow of the Chilean government of Allende forgotten. The campaign of the right to return to the policies of the Cold War soon found fertile ground. Seizing upon the political weakness of the Carter administration, brought on by the failure to resolve the hostage crisis in Iran, enraged by the application of the "Breshnev doctrine" to Afghanistan, it succeeded in reversing the Nixon-Carter foreign policy. In its last year, the Carter administration initiated what we may call Cold War II. Capitulating to the right wing, it made a last minute attempt to derail the Nicaraguan revolution; it declared the Persian Gulf a U.S. preserve; it launched a program of massive rearmament; it virtually ended normal relations with the Soviet Union.

The Reagan administration embraced this program and enlarged upon it. The arms race—which had given some signs that reason would prevail with Salt I and II—has exploded to a level that makes all previous military expenditures look puny in comparison. For the Reagan administration, Angola, Cuba, Nicaragua, El Salvador, Honduras, Guatemala, Cambodia, Afghanistan, the Philippines, and South Africa have become front line states. Even Pol Pot's forces, which exterminated millions of their countrypeople in Cambodia, will now receive their share of U.S. largesse. Military bluster has become the norm, with the basing of nuclear missiles that can annihilate the administrative and economic centers of the Soviet Union in 6, not 30, minutes. Presumably, we will have 24 minutes to cheer the annihilation of the Soviet Union before we too are obliterated. Star Wars has been initiated, a program that, if successful, will provide the United States with first strike capability. (This, of course, is another of Reagan's illusions. Star Wars will not change the balance of power, any more than did our temporary monopoly of, first, the atom bomb, and later the hydrogen bomb. It merely guarantees an escalation of the arms race as the Soviet Union develops appropriate countermeasures.) The moderate Carter policy that led to the agreement on the Panama Canal has been scuttled as the United States descends upon Central America with unprecedented force.

Of even greater concern is the evidence that the Reagan administration is reviving a notion that had a brief acceptance in the 1950s. Containment is not enough, roll-back—i.e., establishing pro-U.S. governments in Soviet-controlled territory, as in Afghanistan—has been given renewed consideration. George Shultz has stated, "We take as part of our obligation to peace to encourage the gradual evolution of the Soviet system toward a more pluralistic political and economic system."

In contrast, particularly after the Vietnam war, the Soviet Union, perhaps convinced of the futility of the Cold War, concerned with the growing disparity between its military and economic strength and that of the United States, concentrated on its own security. No longer are the words of Khrushchev—"We will bury you"—shouted with such arrogant self-confidence at the United Nations, repeated in the Soviet media. In their place is a reduction of aid to left-leaning governments. No Soviet aid was committed to Nicaragua, for instance, until the United States organized the contras.

Even now this aid is small, with the Soviet Union ranking fourth among Nicaragua's trading partners. Help for Ethiopia is minuscule compared to what the United States gives to Somalia, Egypt, Israel, and the Sudan. In Angola, the Soviet Union fights a holding action, careful not to use its troops to oppose the incursion of the highly sophisticated army of South Africa, which coordinates its Angolan war with a South African version of our Nicaraguan Contras.

While the Soviet Union adheres to "proletarian internationalism" and continues its support for national liberation movements, material aid is sharply reduced. Moscow appears content to allow third world revolutions to succeed or fail largely on their own. Even a successful revolution, they have learned to their chagrin, does not mean support for the policy of the Soviet Union: witness China. Clearly, the hopes the Soviet Union may have had in 1945 for the socialization of the world under its leadership have been put on the back burner. In their place is a stream of appeals for a relaxation of tensions, for a return to détente. Serious and meaningful proposals for disarmament are floated by Moscow almost every day. For the first time a superpower has declared a unilateral ban on atom bomb testing, a ban that the Soviet Union promises will continue indefinitely should the United States join in an easily verified agreement. The Soviet Union has made a proposal to cut nuclear arms by 50 percent in five years. The importance of these actions is made obvious by the panic they have created in Washington. Even the Great Communicator cannot convince the people of the world that these are merely Gorbachev public relations ploys. Sooner or later his response, or that of some other President, will have to be substantive.

Though the bluster of the Reagan administration continues unabated, there is growing evidence that his Cold War II policies are in trouble, even without Gorbachev's aid. Latin American governments, burdened by an impossible debt, with inflation of 100 percent per year commonplace, with the U.S. economic revival of the 1980s leaving them untouched, are compelled to develop survival programs. These of necessity weaken the influence of international capital, capital that is overwhelmingly from the United States in origin. A debt revolution is in the offing, and, significantly, representatives from the entire spectrum of political viewpoints—left, right, and middle—met in Cuba to formulate strategy. Suddenly, and unexpectedly, representatives of Brazil, Argentina, Peru, and Uruguay meet with the Contadora nations of Panama, Mexico, Venezuela, and Columbia, urging the United States to enter into negotiations with Nicaragua in a development that calls into question continued U.S. dominance of Latin America.

Nor is the deterioration of U.S. influence limited to Latin America. In Africa, in the Philippines, the wars of liberation grow more intense and widespread. The impact on world opinion of the administration's support for the repression of the blacks in South Africa is at least as damaging as Poland and Afghanistan are to the Soviet Union. The need to chart a new road, one that accepts and even helps the development of an independent Latin America, the need to nurture, not destroy, the independence movements throughout the third world, becomes central to the viability of U.S. influence in the world.

In short, it has become apparent after six years of Cold War II that Reagan's program subverts U.S. interests, something that is recognized by many who oppose him on other than humanitarian or religious grounds. A significant and powerful group of policy-makers, some who presided over Cold War I, openly express this concern. Included are George Kennan, the famous Mr. X; Admiral Stanfield Turner, former head of the CIA, who has called Reagan's Central American policy "state-supported terrorism"; General Nutting, commander-in-chief of our rapid deployment force, who urges that we live with Nicaragua as we do with Cuba; McGeorge Bundy, National Security Advisor to President Kennedy, who warns of the deterioration in U.S. prestige; and many in Congress who await a public outcry before they voice their true feelings. Increasingly, the shibboleths of the past are ignored. There is a growing understanding that for the superpowers the Cold War is nothing more than running hard to stay in one place, while the third world has long recognized that it imposes poverty and a rising death toll. It is heartening that realpolitik and humanitarian considerations coincide. It suggests a broad base upon which a new U.S. foreign policy can be built.

Though after almost five years of the reign of the cold warrior incarnate, Cold War II seems as unsuccessful as its predecessor, its dangers are by no means small. The obsessive pursuit of a failed policy can yet result in ultimate disaster, to say nothing of the death and destruction that its implementation imposes on the people of the third world. But we wear blinders if we cannot see beyond the savagery in Central America and South Africa. Reagan's program is in trouble, but it will not self-destruct. It must be defeated, a responsibility that falls most heavily on the people of the United States. If this attempt to reinstitute the past is defeated, if the policies of the most committed of the cold warriors fail, we open the door to the alternative: instead of colonial wars with their ever present danger of the grand holocaust, a period of détente, of disarmament, and the possibility of economic progress for the poor nations of the earth.

# MARCUS G. RASKIN

Co-founder and Senior Fellow,
Institute for Policy Studies, Washington, D.C.

We have had forty years of the Cold War. And we have thought there could be nothing other than the Cold War. One of the great scientists of the twentieth century, Leo Szilard, once said that when people are at war they cannot imagine peace. So it is with a cold war. It is hard to imagine a peace which is not based on the obviously insane and criminal notions of threatening the destruction of each other's society. So the discussion we need is to imagine alternatives to Cold War which take account of the different ideological systems and which assume the obvious, namely, that so long as life exists on the planet, ideological systems will have to bend to real life problems. Of course, our major problem is the war system itself. Even a founding Cold Warrior, George Kennan, has made it clear that the only way we are able to get rid of nuclear weapons is to get rid of the war system. This may appear to be wildly utopian and idealistic, but as we approach the end of the twentieth century the utopians are those who think that the nation state, and especially the superpowers, can continue on the present course without anything going awry. Imagine a generation from now, assume that there has not been a war, that both sides have gone ahead with the Strategic Defense Initiative (SDI), having spent a trillion dollars, imagine other nations now feeling that they too must have their own deterrent and nuclear strike force against their own enemies, imagine a Japan armed with nuclear weapons and a Germany also so armed, imagine the Middle Eastern nations threatening each other with low- and high-level intensity weapons, imagine that each nation to control its population and to get taxes out of them must greatly increase internal security and police control. Imagine a world where leaders are afraid of making mistakes and governments are expected to be superhuman to avoid mistakes. Is the development of a superhumanly controlled and managed war system possible? If we keep going down the present course, people will have to become rational supermen. But alas this is neither possible nor desirable. Hopefully, as humans we will reject acting like beasts or developing social-technological systems that encourage beastliness. Since we are human we can count on making mistakes. Indeed, it may be that the most we have to give the next generation is the right to make its own mistakes; but when we say we want to have a world where there can be no accident, miscalculation, or mistake, we are denying the young their humanity. This is what we are heading for if we continue down the present path.

There are three stark choices which we are faced with. The first is to keep going as we have been, stumbling forward, playing for tactical advantage, seeing each other in quite inhuman terms as the hated Other who stands for all that is evil in the world. Each side uses freedom, socialism, and democracy as weapons in the struggle for power of one nation state against another. Power grows out of the number of missiles one side has, or the number of tanks, bombs, or soldiers. But history is a harsh teacher, whether in Vietnam or Afghanistan. In the United States, the more weapons we have, the more insecure we become. And the more weapons we create, the more and more difficult to tame are the sorts of institutions that create them. Stumbling forward as we have been is not enough, and it is not enough to have an arms control regimen which takes us back to the endless discussions around SALT, claiming that there is an arms control process when that process is little more than a fig leaf for the two sides to continue their arming game.

The second solution is to assert, wrongly I believe, that the arms race is a technical question. Those who hold to this position would argue that the so-called Star Wars defense, if allowed to proceed by both nations, could result in the abolition of nuclear weapons "through the parallel deployment of defenses in tandem with the incremental reduction of the two arsenals." There is nothing to suggest that this direction would end the arms race or that ways would not be found to avert SDI, or that one side would not fall behind, thereby giving the other side a greater advantage technically—hence increasing the belief that the other side would strike first. There is nothing to suggest that the program itself would not merely increase the militarization of science and totally distort the direction that science could otherwise take. We will be locked into a system in which both sides would be moving in scientific and technical directions perhaps as dangerous and unknown as the beginning of the nuclear age with the tests of A and H bombs—and without any sort of security guarantee. Since the present Star Wars program in the United States is in any case meant to protect weapons and not populations, and since it cannot cover Cruise missiles, Tomahawks, or planes, the SDI can only give some foolish and dangerous policymakers ideas for first strike.

There is a third way, and that is one which I have been and am persuaded must be tried. It is that of common security and general disarmament. What is required for this to become a reality? The first is the suspension of political disbelief in the notion that the problems we face are totally insoluble. Instead we must realize that we have taken a wrong turn surrounded by "a wilderness of proposals," as Professor Louis Sohn has put it, which have a utility only in that they allow the political and mandarin classes of both sides to get together for symbolic discussions.

Where then can we begin? We can develop a program for a generation, or at least one through the year 2000, which is meant to provide a general disarmament and common security regimen between the states. The first task is to realize that the arms race is an astounding exercise in trust. We trust each other's good will and rationality. We assume that we mean the same things by both words. We supposedly value our respective nations in the same way. And if that is so, then perhaps we can move to the next stage, which is the human trust of each other and the realization that our weaponry is outmoded in terms of our needs and that of the world.

We should act on a program of unilateral initiatives which could include a moratorium of nuclear testing, something that should have been done in 1963. We can work out a program of international conduct in the third world and through the United Nations. We can begin an immediate negotiation on a worldwide common security and general disarmament program, which should be completed by 1990 so that by 2000 our nations will be fixed irrevocably to a general disarmament program and to a substantially different system of world politics.

Over the past few years a study group of the Institute for Policy Studies (IPS) and the Soviet Academy of Sciences has initiated a program to this end. Our intention is to reach out to other scholars, organizations, and leaders for their comments and participation in the project. In 1964 Kenneth Boulding, the distinguished social scientist, called for an "invisible college" from around the world to formulate a peace system. This is our intention.

# LEON WOFSY

Professor of Immunology, Emeritus,
University of California, Berkeley

## The Reagan Doctrine and After

Our commentaries on the shape of things to come in the Cold War will be read against a nonstop barrage of new and unprecedented events. From Manila to Tripoli to Chernobyl, momentous happenings continuously break into our conceptions of what the future holds.

The Geneva summit meeting in November 1985, far from winding down the Cold War, marked only a pause before a new crescendo of violence and international tension. The priorities of the Reagan foreign policy have become more visible, and arms control is certainly not among them. There is an aggressive demeanor that asserts confidence in superior U.S. power, but that also manifests increasing impatience with persistent impediments to its freedom of action.

President Reagan's administration has entered the home stretch, highly conscious of the limited time that remains to shape his legacy. The "Reagan Doctrine," previewed in several speeches by Secretary of State George Shultz, has now been proclaimed formally in a presidential message to Congress (*New York Times,* 15 March, 1986). The bombing of Libya, writes Eugene V. Rostow in the *New York Times* of 27 April 1986, is not "an isolated episode . . . confined to the issue of terrorism," but "a breakthrough of incalculable psychological and political importance." It should be viewed, according to Rostow, "in the cold perspective of geopolitics as the first step in carrying out what should be called the Reagan Doctrine."

That doctrine claims the duty to intervene with all "the tools of American policy" in every regional conflict and national political

struggle anywhere in the world. Its most enthusiastic goal is to go
"beyond containment" of Soviet influence to bring about the
downfall of diverse governments categorized as Soviet clients. It
proclaims worldwide "democratic revolution" but the universal
standard laid down is the primacy of the United States in de-
fining and directing every situation. The policy is not lacking in
flexibility: where Duvalier and Marcos absolutely cannot be saved,
hail their departure and maximize the role of friendly generals
in the new order; where hopes of securing the Botha and Chun
regimes remain, reinforce and advise them in their struggle
against the repressed opposition; make life as hard as possible for
every country on the administration's enemies list, supplying
weapons and generalship indiscriminately to all groups willing to
do battle.

Little time elapses these days between horrifying examples of
"human error," the accidents and miscalculations of which disaster is fashioned. But the most ominous miscalculations are strategic: faulty estimates that lend seeming rationality to policies that
risk wars. Describing the administration's decision "to act with
greater freedom and decisiveness around the world," Leslie Gelb
reports (*New York Times*, 5 April 1986): "Behind these judgments
is a new and fundamental consensus in the Administration that
Mr. Reagan has altered the correlation of overall power with
Moscow and that the Russians are 'on the run'. . . ." We are driven
to the memory of past tragedies, when similar appraisals of Soviet
weakness merged with messianic anti-Communism!

So, to the surprise of few, these last years of the Reagan
presidency will severely test the limits of U.S.-Soviet confrontation. Can the Reagan Doctrine prevail? How can or will the Soviets
respond? Will the approaching end of Reagan's tenure alter prospects for curbing the Cold War?

Putting the question directly—about the possibility of a peaceful
turn away from the Cold War—is somehow unsettling. It brings
out differences, shown by the responses in this volume, about how
one understands "Cold War," how one views each adversary, how
one conceives of "détente"—indeed, how one looks at the world.
It might be easier to approach consensus if the opposite query had
been put: Is it possible the Cold War could end in catastrophe? But

that heavy question has been asked and answered by most of us. This editorial comment focuses rather on issues of controversy among the contributors to our book, the set of difficult questions that shape our answer to the main question—is a peaceful ending achievable?

The first issue, put forward by Strobe Talbott and others, is what is meant by the term Cold War. Is "Cold War" simply a euphemism for U.S.-Soviet rivalry? Martin Sherwin writes: "I do not think that the Cold War can be distinguished from the U.S.-Soviet rivalry; by definition that rivalry is the Cold War." The contrary view, which I share with Stanley Hoffmann and George Breslauer, is that the differences between U.S. and Soviet society are basic and enduring, but that these neither define the Cold War nor make it inevitable. If the condition for ending the Cold War is termination of the rivalry, the outlook would seem as hopeless as it is terrifying.

While all aspects of U.S.-Soviet relations are affected, the Cold War can be defined by two distinguishing features. The first is an arms race at levels that surpass the capacity for eliminating life on earth, a competition unlimited by any serious negotiations or effective mutual efforts for arms control. The second is a level of hostility so intense that it engulfs all international and domestic problems, especially every third world conflict, and subordinates them to the U.S.-Soviet antagonism.

By that definition, ending the Cold War does not mean ending historic differences between U.S. and Soviet society, but depriving them of the particularly intense and deadly form they have assumed in the nuclear age. It means achieving conditions in which the arms race can be stopped and defanged of the instant capacity for world annihilation, and in which the Great Contest is no longer so dominant as to distort and suppress all other concerns. That is ambitious enough, but it may not be beyond reach over the next couple of decades.

The issues that most sharply divide our contributors have to do with estimating the nature and depth of commitment of either or both of the superpowers to the Cold War system. Some consider that the very nature of Soviet ideology and society is the source of the conflict (Flora Lewis), some that the Reagan administration spearheads the Cold War whereas current Soviet leadership desires a return to détente (Robert Scheer, Hans Bethe, Malcolm Gordon, and others), some that differences between both sides are far less basic than the dependence of each on the other to provide the Great Satan with which to justify its own foreign and domestic policies (Noam Chomsky, E. P. Thompson).

For me the most distressing response to our question on the possibility for ending the Cold War came from Noam Chomsky— not only because it is so absolute in its pessimism, but also because I have great respect for the author and a case he argues is never easily dismissed. He maintains that both societies require the Cold War system, that neither the U.S. nor the Soviet leadership will give it up, and that "the prospect of a terminal war, one of the ever present elements of this system, [is] an increasing likelihood." Of course, this analysis is not invalidated by virtue of its hopelessness. Yet it can hardly be accepted without challenge by any who conceive that the struggle for peace is realistic, that it is not simply a measure of morality in a world doomed to succumb to what E. P. Thompson has called "exterminism."

Must we assume that leaderships and policies committed to a drastic change in the warlike climate cannot prevail in either the United States or the Soviet Union? That implies an estimate of each society that is, in my opinion, too fixed and too undifferentiated.

The view among some left critics that no U.S. president will break with the Cold War emphasizes, first, the heavy economic dependence of the military-industrial complex on the arms race, and second, the essentially bipartisan character of U.S. foreign policy commitments to the Cold War and to the dominance of U.S. interests around the world. What is generally underestimated, however, are the increasingly critical problems inherent in the unyielding pursuit of such a course, the divisions it fosters, the resistance it confronts in a world threatened by nuclear holocaust. Even the Reagan administration, despite its upbeat stance, has to struggle and maneuver repeatedly to maintain the pace of the military build-up and to avoid significant steps toward arms control. Despite Rambo mania, ambivalence has appeared in President Reagan's public posture toward relations with the "evil empire," and he has acknowledged that no one can win a nuclear war. In his inimitable style, after years of denying the value of summit meetings he now seeks to exploit summitry as evidence that his warlike conduct is inspired by peaceful intentions. This does not indicate that the President is preparing to give up on the Cold War, or even, as some see it, that the administration has no foreign policy. It does suggest that U.S. policy, despite the Reagan Doctrine, has not been made immune to challenge or change.

There is good reason to take serious account, as Robert Scheer does, of pressures within our society and worldwide for a more realistic and less dangerous course. The biggest initial tests of the move to more assertive behavior under the Reagan Doctrine—the bombing of Libya and the demand for $100 million for the Contra war against Nicaragua—produced some reactions and results that departed markedly from expectations. If the administration set out to display a new lack of inhibition in its resort to acts of war, it proved even more that it can recruit very few partners for such enterprises. It was also proved, in the aftermath of the Libyan demonstration, that massive military terror only increases the incidence of retaliatory terrorist acts. At home, in contrast to international reaction, the attack on Libya won the anticipated cheers that are always the short-term response when a nation's glorious armed forces strike an adversary. More remarkable, however, was that the wave of jingoism did not perceptibly change public opposition to aid for the Contra war against Nicaragua. Certainly the minds of most of the citizenry have been turned to a Cold War view of the Sandinistas. Yet the full force of the President's popularity, inflammatory concoctions, and his arm-twisting of Congress and the press does not banish the "Vietnam syndrome" from public consciousness. Even less does it diminish opposition in Latin America or elsewhere in the world to the military "solution" sought by the administration. Nicaragua's fate is uncertain; but the unrealistic calendar for getting rid of the Cuban as well as Nicaraguan governments—declared a top priority by Alexander Haig and Eugene Rostow at the very beginning of Reagan's first term—has become historic testimony to rising limitations on the effectiveness of military power.

The Reagan presidency has not been simply a continuation of "bipartisan consensus" but a crusade to reinvigorate the Cold War by going over to the offensive and restoring "roll-back" ambitions of John Foster Dulles vintage. While the book may be far from closed on the Democrats' contributions to the Cold War system—accurately recounted in Martin Sherwin's commentary—disaffection with policies of unending military build-up and nuclear confrontation is unmistakable and its political potential is powerful.

One may marvel at or bemoan the Reagan phenomenon, but the ultimate success or failure of the crusade is still to be decided. Squeezing the Soviet Union by forcing military and technological competition to the extreme puts the squeeze on our economic and political vulnerabilities as well. Almost halfway into the Reagan second term, one may question whether the image of a Soviet military threat can remain sufficiently inflated to provide a permanent rationale for enormous burdens and risks. In fact, that rationale has not sufficed in the short run to gain the combination of domestic and international acquiescence necessary to overthrow the Sandinistas and to stabilize "loyal" regimes facing massive popular opposition. These last years of the Reagan administration will not see a "peaceful ending," but they may decide how much enthusiasm there will be for continuing the great gamble much longer.

The view that the government of the Soviet Union relies on the Cold War to sustain its control at home and in Eastern Europe also ignores the pressures in Soviet society for relief from the burdens of the arms race, the fear of nuclear war, and the swamp of a politically and morally debilitating war in Afghanistan. The Chernobyl disaster must add to the sense that change is urgent. It is a terrible stimulus to consciousness—for us as much as for the Soviet Union—of the dependence of human survival on a new standard of international cooperation, openness, and responsibility.

Whatever the contending currents in Soviet life and development, evidence points to a dominant desire for détente, for turning down the arms race and averting its spread into space. Moreover, as George Breslauer suggests, we may be witnessing one of the "key turning points in the development of Soviet politics when there is a greater openness or space for political innovation, a demonstrated inclination to innovate in the direction of holding down the rate of growth of military expenditures and making certain types of concessions in order to harness the arms race."

There is an obvious effort to replace rigidity with initiative in Gorbachev's proposals for a drastic reduction of nuclear and conventional armaments, especially in the prolonged unilateral moratorium on nuclear weapons tests. This seems to run counter to the suggestion of Michael MccGwire that the Soviet Union may have already concluded, toward the end of the first Reagan administration, that U.S. hostility was so deeply rooted that the long-term competitive "struggle would have to be waged primarily in the political-military arena."

Diana Johnstone points out that polarization between pro-U.S. and pro-Soviet positions is far less true of international political forces today than during the first Cold War in the 1950s. Certainly the independence of major peace movements from the policies of either superpower is demonstrable. Inevitably there are different judgments among peace activists in all countries on the nature and complexities of both societies. A characteristic of the Cold War climate, however, is that judgments become so absolute that they bar recognition of factors in one or the other society that make possible a more peaceful and humane course.

A very difficult question for peace activists in the Western world, especially in the United States, is to sort out the ways in which the problems of human rights and the right of self-determination become entangled with attitudes to the Cold War. Most who actively oppose the arms race have no inclination to be silent about human rights abuses or intervention against weaker nations, whether the target of criticism is the United States, the Soviet union, or allies of either. Striving for détente should be no excuse for putting such issues on hold, although these problems certainly will remain and will demand active concern even if the Cold War recedes.

The picture gets pushed out of focus, I believe, when movement toward détente is *itself* conceived as compromising the causes of human rights and self-determination and undermining struggles against oppression in the third world. To see more peaceful U.S.-Soviet relations as "a system of joint global management by the two superpowers" (Chomsky) implies that forces for social change can be called on or off by Reagan or Gorbachev or both. Reagan's "hot spots" in Central America are not due to Gorbachev, and cannot be

extinguished with his hypothetical cooperation; the main problems in Eastern Europe are not manufactured in the United States
and will not be settled in the unlikely event that a U.S. President
calls off the CIA. What détente does require is restraints on
provocative behavior, especially military interventionism. While
both superpowers may get serious about avoiding dangerous confrontation, neither is able—much less willing—to underwrite the
other's "area of domination" or to insure it against domestic unrest.

Nevertheless, there is a likely consequence of easing tensions
that harbors discomfort for worshippers of the status quo: to the
extent that the Cold War rationale is ruptured, the base of support
within either society for suppressive measures and strident militarism must, on balance, be weakened. In particular, it would be
harder, not easier, to muster support for military actions against
third world countries or to isolate them from international assistance. The fear that the third world may be subjugated via
superpower collusion not only underestimates basic differences
between the United States and the Soviet Union, but it may also
overlook the central reality that we have passed the time in history
when even an imaginary "super superpower" could control the
turbulent processes underway in the third world.

Sorting these issues out is complicated by the overriding sweep
of anti-Sovietism in our politics and culture. Is this phenomenon
a valid concern? Is it distinguishable per se from expressions
of opposition to Soviet military action in Afghanistan, suppression of Solidarity in Poland, or repression of dissidents in the Soviet
Union?

In its crudest form, prominent in movie and comic strip fantasies, anti-Sovietism is war propaganda. However, the phenomenon
is also operative as an intimidating influence against any view that
is not unreservedly hostile toward Soviet society or that rejects the
orthodox representation of the "Soviet threat to the free world."
Even among critics of our foreign and military policies, to remain
within the pale seems to require repetitious proof of antagonism to
the Soviet Union. There is a conditioned reflex to ignore or
condemn as insincere any Soviet proposal indicating a desire to
turn the arms race downward. There is a reflexive fear of being
"soft on Communism" if one doubts that our national security is

jeopardized by the existence of the Sandinista government or by the destabilization of anti-Communist regimes, even those of Botha and Pinochet. Small wonder that a real debate on policy toward the Soviet Union is missing from Congress and from national politics generally.

This imposed conformity also inhibits thought and discussion on questions of world outlook and political philosophy beyond the specific consideration of U.S.-Soviet relations. Although not a major topic in the forum represented by this book, problems of ideology were touched on by several contributors. Paul Sweezy argues that underlying the causes of the Cold War "is a fundamental hostility of capitalism to the very existence of an alternative social system which is both viable on its own terms and able to resist penetration and absorption into the capitalist world order." Tom Wicker, from a different point of view, raised a similar question: "Will the United States be willing in the years ahead to tolerate Marxist governments in the Western hemisphere if they arise, or are we going to take the attitude that that is the one thing that we will not tolerate?"

One effect of the Cold War is that ideological differences about the course of human development are projected in terms of "our" way of life (in the United States) versus "their" way of life (in the Soviet Union). Anti-Sovietism serves then not only to deny anything positive in the experience, influence, and potential of Soviet society, but systematically to generalize its negative features as a global indictment of all Marxist ideas and all experiments in socialism. This is no small matter simply to be absorbed as an uncomfortable fact of life in U.S. politics. Not only does it retard any understanding of and with the Soviet Union, but it alienates the United States from the growing number of countries struggling for new ways of social and economic organization—often against pressures, punishments, and harsh criticisms that make independence from U.S. economic and political power an extremely precarious endeavor.

To return to the main theme, it seems to me that neither the ideologies nor the wish lists of U.S. and Soviet leaders are the primary consideration for evaluating whether peaceful termination of the Cold War is a real possibility in the foreseeable future.

The determining factor is whether the realities of the world of today and tomorrow are compelling enough not to be denied past the point of no return. Fundamentally that depends on people, their insistence in overwhelming numbers that the threat to life on earth be lifted. For populations on both sides of the Cold War, the calamitous accidents of 1986 have to weigh more heavily than advances and fantasies in the realm of space and nuclear technology. Increasingly governments may find it necessary to adjust to limitations on past ambitions that can never be made viable by any amount of Cold War fervor or accumulated military capacity. Moreover, as it becomes impossible to hide or postpone economic difficulties, popular priorities and conceptions may be altered in ways considered in Manning Marable's contribution. As Stanley Hoffmann has suggested, "the Cold War could come to a peaceful end from the bottom, so to speak, rather than from the top, if each of the two rivals gets increasingly concerned with its own domestic problems and finds itself giving priority abroad to issues in which the chief rival plays only an insignificant role."

Possibilities are not promises or predictions. None of us need be reminded that the worst scenario may await us. But possibilities have to be recognized in order for them to be fought for and realized.